Statistical Models in
Behavioral Research

William K. Estes
Harvard University

LAWRENCE ERLBAUM ASSOCIATES, PUBLISHERS
1991   Hillsdale, New Jersey   Hove and London

BF
39
.E72
1991

Lawrence Erlbaum Associates, Inc., Publishers
365 Broadway
Hillsdale, New Jersey 07642

Library of Congress Cataloging-in-Publication Data

Estes, William Kaye.
    Statistical models in behavioral research / W.K. Estes.
        p.   cm.
    Includes bibliographical references and index.
    ISBN 0-8058-0686-5 (cloth). — ISBN 0-8058-0688-1 (pbk.)
    1. Psychometrics.   2. Psychology—Research.   3. Psychology-
Statistical methods.   4. Psychology—Mathematical models.
I. Title.
BF39.E72   1991
150'.1'5195—dc20   90-43392
                                                                                              CIP

Printed in the United States of America
10 9 8 7 6 5 4 3 2 1

For George and Rhey

Contents

Preface

This book evolved during my teaching of courses in statistics and quantitative methods to advanced undergraduate and graduate students in psychology and social science off and on for nearly 40 years. Apologies are due the students who happened to fall in earlier classes, before I had learned how to teach this kind of material effectively, and appreciation is due to many collaborators and assistants. In the latter connection, I owe a special debt to Robert R. Rosenthal, with whom I shared a graduate course at Harvard University for 8 years and from whom I have learned a good deal about how to help students get across the gap between theory and application. I also want to mention a succession of outstanding teaching assistants at Harvard, including Beverly Chew, Jean MacMillan, and most notably, Kris Kirby, who caught seemingly innumerable glitches in draft chapters of this volume and brought my attention to many possibilities for improving communicability. Finally, I wish to thank Nancy Rury, who accomplished the all but impossible task of converting my handwritten drafts into neat typescript, Kay Estes, who prepared the index, and my longtime friend and publisher, Lawrence Erlbaum, who personally supervised the final transition from typescript into print.

W. K. E.

1 Introduction

WHAT IS NEW?

The teacher of a graduate course in statistics for psychologists or other behavioral scientists now has so many excellent texts available (for example, Hays, 1988; Hildebrand, 1986; Howell, 1987; Kirk, 1982; Loftus & Loftus, 1988) that one may well ask, "Why should another be needed?" The atypically small size of this volume may suggest the answer: I set out to supplement, not to duplicate, available textbooks. I assume that the reader has had or is taking a course that covers the elements of probability, sampling distributions, and the computation of analyses of variance and regression on balanced data sets obtained from simple, standard designs. I assume further that the reader shares with this author at least the following needs:

1. Capability of doing statistical analyses by means of statistical programs with some insight into what is going on behind the scenes.
2. Understanding of the basis for the various rules given in textbooks about admissable tests in various common designs.
3. Guidance in the calculation and use of statistics never fully covered in standard texts (e.g., effect size measures, standard errors, and contrasts in various types of designs).

4. Deeper insight into the relationship between analysis of variance and regression and the ways of getting the best of both approaches out of statistical packages.
5. Help in dealing with the hazards of unbalanced data sets.

The state of the art in statistics for psychological research is changing rapidly and with it what the researcher needs to learn. The prototype of a second course for prospective research workers in behavioral science is a concentration on mastering methods of calculating analyses of variance (henceforth ANOVAs) for a variety of common research designs. However, the hand calculation of ANOVAs is rapidly going out of style. Often (unhappily), even before learning a modicum of statistics, the student in psychology enters research data into computer programs and then seeks help in decoding a massive output of summary tables. The reward is a large increase in output for a given amount of time and effort on the input side. The negative aspect is similar to that of putting powerful machines into untrained hands. The ability to obtain statistical analyses soon outruns the ability to interpret them. Thus, the present-day student needs more theory than his predecessors were even allowed to see in order to be able to cope with the outputs of computer programs.

Meeting these needs requires some understanding of the models that underlie statistical methods and how the models can be applied to guide the solution of new problems not covered by textbook examples. However, although the mathematics needed for practical purposes is not very deep, the difficulties of coping with mathematical formalisms and details of derivations have tended to make the needed approach inaccessible to all but a few behavioral scientists. In this connection, I have been struck by the findings of current research in cognitive science that the early development of children's understanding of science and mathematics is greatly facilitated if the qualitative understanding of physical or mathematical models precedes the task of dealing with computational details. Thus, I have wondered whether it may be possible to convey the essentials of statistical models by means of simplified representations that eliminate most of the complexities of notation and focus on qualitative understanding of the models. An individual who learns to think in terms of models in this way will not be able to do much in the way of new derivations for novel problems but perhaps will be equipped to find his/her way intelligently through many of the difficulties of interpreting research data and in particular to reap the advantages of statistical packages with some confidence in how to interpret the outputs.

I have no magic bullet to offer, but over many years of teaching research design and quantitative methods in psychology, I have developed some ways of simplifying the presentations of concepts and derivations so as to make the substance of important statistical results available to the mathematically unskilled research worker. An important boost to this effort has come quite recently in the appearance of some readily available microcomputer programs, most notably SYSTAT, that encourage, even in some instances require, the user to plan the analysis of a statistical design in relation to the mathematical model that underlies the computations. In this book, I follow a path somewhere between the level of the SYSTAT manual (Wilkinson, 1986), in which models appear only in the form of highly simplified and stylized equations that serve as instructions to the program, and that of treatises like Winer (1971), in which models are presented fully but with so much detail of notation and derivation as to be inaccessible to all but a few users.

There is no new statistical theory in this book. The basic theory I have drawn on is well covered in Graybill (1961), Searle (1987), and Winer (1971). My contribution has been mostly to abstract, reorganize, and apply the theoretical results to problems that arise frequently in psychological research and especially to find ways of simplifying the presentation of models and operations with models so as to make them readily available to students and investigators who lack either mathematical background or taste for doing derivations, or both. For the experienced investigator, I include material on model testing and related topics that is not covered in textbooks or other readily available sources.

A COMPARISON OF STATISTICAL AND SCIENTIFIC MODELS

My view of statistical models and their applications as simply a special case of the uses of formal models in scientific theory and research may seem unconventional to some readers. The close relationship of the two types of models can, however, be pointed out in terms of an illustration. A simple theoretical model that has become very familiar in cognitive psychology is the function relating reaction time to set size in short-term memory search. In a paradigm made famous by Sternberg (1966), an experimental subject is presented with a small set of items, typically randomly selected digits, letters, or short words, then is presented with a test item and responds yes or no as quickly as possible, yes indicating that the test item was in the set of items presented (the memory set) and no indicating that it was not. On the assumption that the memory set is represented in the subject's short-term memory system in a list-like format and that the task of responding to the test item is achieved by comparing it successively to each of the items in the memory representation, reaction time for the yes or no response can be predicted from the function

$$Y = a + bi \tag{1.1}$$

where Y denotes mean reaction time to respond to the test item, a is the time required to generate a response, b is the time required for a single comparison of the test item with an item in memory, and i is the number of items in the set.

This scientific hypothesis seems straightforward, but how are we to decide whether or not it is supported by data? The upper panel in FIG. 1.1 presents the problem more concretely. The open squares in the figure represent data from a hypothetical memory search experiment in the form of mean reaction time at each set size, and the straight line represents the theoretical hypothesis with a particular choice of values of the constants *a* and *b*. It appears to the eye that the data and the hypothesis are in fair agreement, but for many scientific purposes one wishes to be able to say something more specific and preferably quantitative about the goodness of fit. In the course of research in this paradigm, investigators have, for example, wanted to make comparisons of the goodness of fit in different studies that have used different kinds of items, different conditions of item presentation, or the like, or they have wanted to compare the goodness of fit of this hypothesis with others that differ from it in some particular way. To serve these purposes, it is necessary to replace our initial general and somewhat vague statement of the problem of goodness of fit with more structured and specific questions to which definite answers can be obtained.

To start this process, we note that the data points in FIG. 1.1 do not fall on the plotted straight line exactly but vary somewhat irregularly around it. This result is to be expected if there is experimental error in the situation so that different experimental subjects differ somewhat from each other in performance and so that the reaction times obtained from a particular subject on a particular set size may vary somewhat from one occasion to another. Thus, we need to face the question whether we can confidently rule out the possibility that the upward trend of the data points in FIG. 1.1 is simply a chance result of the error in the situation. Two steps that we take in order to deal with this question are illustrated in the middle panel of FIG. 1.1. The first step is to augment the equation for the theoretical hypothesis by a term, e, representing experimental error. We have, in a manner of speaking, imbedded the theoretical model in a statistical model, in particular a linear regression

FIG. 1.1 Steps in statistically evaluating a scientific hypothesis. The upper panel presents a set of observed data in the form of mean reaction times versus size of a set of items to be remembered (in an experimental paradigm described in the text) together with a theoretical hypothesis that takes the form of a linear function relating reaction time to set size.

For a first test of the hypothesis, it is compared with the simpler hypothesis that reaction time is constant over set size, represented by the horizontal line in the middle panel. If the result of the first test demonstrates a significant positive slope for the observed trend, thus rejecting the simpler model, we ask next whether the trend is specifically linear. To answer that question, we compare the model representing the linear trend with the augmented model illustrated in the bottom panel, in which a quantity t is added to or subtracted from the linear function at each set size.

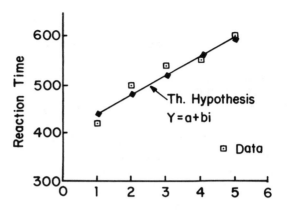

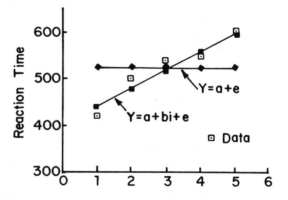

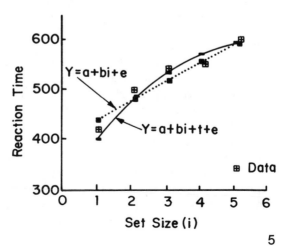

model. The equation for the latter expresses the idea that the observed data should represent a combination of the true theoretical function relating reaction time to set size with an error term that may result in observed points falling randomly above or below the true function at each set size.

The second step is to formulate an alternative hypothesis, represented by the horizontal line and accompanying regression equation in the middle panel of FIG. 1.1, expressing the possibility that there is no true relation between reaction time and set size and that the observed trend might be simply a combination of a horizontal straight line plus random error. As will be described in detail in Chapter 7, a computer program for regression analysis, given the full set of data values as input, will form an estimate of the magnitude of experimental error, select values of constants a and b that are the best possible in the sense that they reduce the variability of the data points around the theoretical function to a minimum, and will enable us to make a quantitative statement about the confidence with which we can conclude that the upward sloping function provides a better account of the data than the horizontal function.

If the results of this analysis enable us to conclude that the upward trend in the data points is real (i.e., not due to chance) so that the scientific hypothesis is preferable to the alternative one, we may wish to proceed to the specific question whether the particular assumption of a linear relation between reaction time and set size, assumed in the theoretical hypothesis, provides a better description of the data than some alternative function that would have an upward trend of a different form, such as the curvilinear function shown in the bottom panel of FIG. 1.1. At various times in the history of research in this paradigm, investigators have in fact surmised that the true relation is better assumed to be a logarithmic or power function than a straight line.

In order to be able to make a decision about these alternative functions as a class, we define the statistical model represented by the lowermost equation in FIG. 1.1, which will be seen to be the linear regression function plus an additional term t. The values of t, which in general would be different from one set size to another, represent the differences between the values predicted by the augmented hypothesis and the values predicted by the linear hypothesis. Working in the regression framework, we do not attempt to guess what the values of t should be but rather let the statistical computer program determine the values that are best in the sense of yielding the smallest *error estimate*, that is, the smallest variation of the observed data points around the function. The final step is to compare this error estimate for the linear and the augmented hypothesis and produce a quantitative statement as to whether the augmented model yields a significantly better account of the data than the linear model.[1]

The specific statistical concepts and tools needed to understand how the regression program accomplishes these purposes will be developed in the next few chapters. At this point, I wish only to emphasize the overall strategy of imbedding the idealized relationship derived from a scientific hypothesis (as the one expressed in Equation 1.1) in a model general enough to allow for the possibility that either this hypothesis or some alternative hypothesis is true. One can then determine in a systematic way whether the hypothesized relation or the alternative is better justified by the data. This strategy of comparing a more general model with a simpler one that is in a sense included within it underlies all of the types of statistical hypothesis testing that will be covered in this volume.

ORGANIZATION OF THE VOLUME

The following four chapters develop the tools needed to understand a variety of ANOVA and regression designs and the models underlying them. These chapters review the elements of probability and decision theory, sampling distributions, contrast analysis, and hypothesis testing. The tools are then applied to a sample of research problems chosen to illustrate the various aspects of design and analysis represented in the following outline, all of the treatments being integrated within a common theoretical framework known in the statistical literature as the *general linear model*.

Balanced Designs
    Fixed effects
        One-way ANOVA
        Simple regression
        Multiple classifications
            ANOVAs
            Mixed ANOVA and regression
    Random effects
        One-way ANOVA
        Intra-class correlation

---

[1]As will be seen in Chapter 7, this technique is not limited to the case where a scientific hypothesis prescribes a linear function but can be generalized to any specified function.

Mixed models, including repeated measures
  Two-way ANOVAs
  Two-way ANOVA/Regression
  Higher order and nested designs
Multiple regression and analysis of covariance
Unbalanced Designs

For most purposes, we can take "balanced design" to denote one in which all cells contain equal numbers of scores, although there are a few infrequently occurring exceptional cases that qualify (see Howell, 1987, p. 392). Imbalance raises no special problems for one-way designs, but for two-way and higher-order classifications, the distinction between balanced and unbalanced designs is critical. The familiar algebraic breakdown of a total sum of squares into components associated with main effects, interactions, and error; the property of ANOVA tables that the component sums of squares add up to the total sum of squares; the obvious correspondence of F tests to simply stateable hypotheses about population parameters—all hold only for balanced designs. Therefore, I defer the problem of dealing with unbalanced designs for special treatment at the end of the tour.

My treatment of methods and designs stops short of multivariate analysis of variance (MANOVA). One reason is that in order to concentrate on mathematical reasoning rather than derivations, I limit the mathematics used in the book to simple algebra, eschewing even matrix operations. A second reason is that there are many presentations of MANOVA available (e.g., Dunteman, 1984; Finn, 1974; Harris, 1985) that are fully adequate for courses on multivariate methods and for the needs of investigators who work with predominantly correlational data. With this limitation, it has been possible to give a compact but reasonably complete presentation of the basic statistical models needed by investigators whose research is primarily experimental in character and is often oriented toward the testing of quantitative theories.

2 Statistics, Probability, and Decision

GENERAL CONSIDERATIONS

I think it would be hard to find an informed person contesting the proposition that probability theory is basic to statistics. But why do people believe this proposition to be true? An answer suggested by many textbook presentations and by the unending controversies between adherents of different approaches to probability and statistics (Bayesian, Fisherian, etc.) is that the probabilities computed in the course of statistical applications can be regarded as properties of events that occur in the research situations. When the applications are to gambling situations involving, for example, fair coins, dice, or roulette wheels, it is known that probabilities derived from statistical theory do closely describe actual long-term experience and can be ignored by the gambler only at the cost of certain ruin. When the applications are to scientific research situations, however, whether in physical science, agriculture, or social science, I know of no evidence to suggest that the same is true.

Why, then, do scientists in all fields depend heavily on statistical methods based on probability theory? I suggest that the answer is much the same as for other uses of formal models in science. A statistical model for an experiment is a deliberate idealization of the actual empirical situation, and probabilities derived by means of the model hold strictly only for the idealized, not for the actual, situation. In a few instances, such as gambling and perhaps some applications in physical science, the idealized situation of the model may be so close to the empirical one that probabilities derived are literally interpretable as properties of events. In biology, psychology, and social science, however, such correspondences are rare, and there must be other reasons for using statistics and taking derived probabilities to be empirically significant. The only defensible answer, I would say, is that just as with any methods in science, the use of statistical methods is justified by long-term experience. Thus, although there is no reason to think that the probability value derived from application of a statistical test to a psychological experiment tells us how often an observed result would occur in actual research if a hypothesized effect were absent, a large body of experience assures us that, other things equal, a result significant at the .01 level will more often prove replicable than a result significant at the .05 level. In general, relative values of derived probabilities are often highly informative, although absolute values may not be.

The reader should not, however, leap to the conclusion that I am one of those who depreciate the use of conventional significance levels. Quite to the contrary, I think the use of conventional significance levels is useful and entirely defensible, not because the absolute probability values are empirically meaningful, but because the use of conventional significance levels can be conducive to clear thinking. To see why this is so, we need to review a few basic concepts of probability and decision.

OUTCOME TREES AND DECISION CRITERIA

When considering application of statistics to a research situation, the investigator needs routinely to attend to two preliminaries. The first is to consider whether there is reason to believe that the research design includes an element of randomization that would make application of a probability model appropriate. The second, if the answer to the first is affirmative, is to lay out an outcome tree for the experiment and to specify decision criteria.

We say that a set of events is random if the long-term relative frequencies of occurrence of the events over replications of the situation settle down to stable values, and if manipulation of these values according to the laws of probability yields empirically confirmable predictions. We know from experience that these criteria are satisfied by tosses of coins or dice and by the outputs of well-constructed computer programs for the generation of random numbers. Thus, we can and do use these devices to lift ourselves by our boot straps, so to speak, in research situations and introduce the randomness required for appropriate application of statistical models by making random assignments of experimental units to conditions (for example, subjects to groups). When and only when this procedure is properly done, we have reason to believe that the outcomes of replications of an experiment will vary randomly and, therefore, that probabilities can meaningfully be assigned to classes of outcomes.

The second step in preparing for a statistical application is to describe in some way the collection of all possible outcomes of an experiment that could occur over an indefinitely large set of replications. This description of all possible outcomes defines a concept known as the *sample space* in probability theory but that can be denoted more informally as the *outcome tree* for an experiment. Probabilities are assigned to all branches of the outcome tree.

In the case of tossing a fair coin, the outcome tree has just two branches, corresponding to heads and tails, and under the hypothesis of fairness, each branch has probability .5. In the case of tossing a die, the outcome tree has six branches, one corresponding to each possible outcome of a toss, and on the assumption of fairness, each is assigned a probability of 1/6.

A more interesting application of the concept of outcome tree is shown in FIG. 2.1 and illustrates the important point that many problems involving probability are virtually solved once the appropriate outcome tree has been constructed. The tree in FIG. 2.1 represents a hypothetical study intended to evaluate a lie detector test. On the basis of a number of research studies, it is a reasonable assumption that a lie detector with a competent operator will yield a positive test result about 90% of the time for an individual who actually has guilty knowledge and about 50% of the time for an individual who is actually innocent. If the test is applied to a group of subjects 10% of whom are guilty and 90% innocent, then the outcome tree is as represented in FIG. 2.1, the column headed Outcome Probability indicating that a combination of a guilty person and a positive test result occurs 9% of the time, a guilty person with a negative test result 1% of the time, and so on.

Now suppose we wish to answer the highly relevant question: What is the probability that an individual who yields a positive test result is actually guilty? The question could be answered by an appropriate application of Bayes' theorem, but it can be answered even more directly by reference to the outcome tree. To obtain the answer, we simply mask out the branches leading to negative test results, as in FIG. 2.2, and note that the total probability of positive test results is .54, of which .09 is associated with guilty and .45 with innocent persons, so that the probability that a person with a positive test result is actually guilty is equal to .09/(.09 + .45) = .17. This result is surprising to many people,

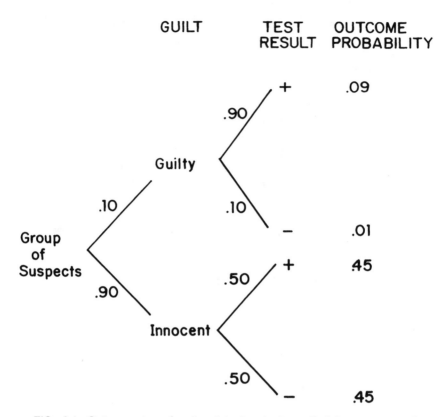

FIG. 2.1. Outcome tree for lie detector test applied to a group of suspects, 10% of whom are guilty and 90% innocent. The right-hand column gives the probabilities of outcomes in which guilty or innocent persons yield positive or negative test results.

because the information that guilty people yield positive test results 90% of the time is apt to create the impression (actually the very misleading impression) that the test is highly efficacious at distinguishing guilt from innocence. Almost equally surprising is the ease with which the problem is solved once the outcome tree is constructed.

When our purpose is to construct a statistical test of a hypothesis, the outcome tree must be augmented by a *decision criterion*. If, for example, we wished to test the fairness of a particular coin, we would choose some number of tosses, say 10, and then the outcome tree would have a branch for each of the 2^{10} possible results of tossing the coin 10 times. We would not write down all of the 2^{10} outcomes of course, but we would proceed directly to classify them in a way appropriate to the hypothesis being

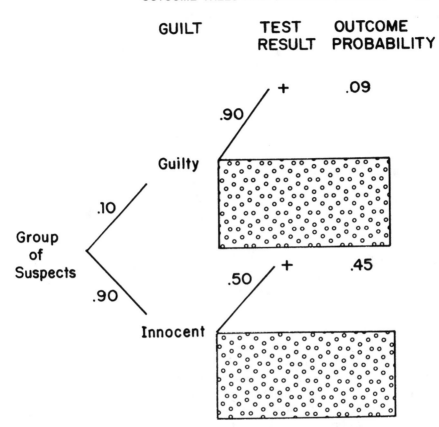

FIG. 2.2. Outcome tree of FIG. 2.1 modified by masking out the outcomes associated with negative test outcomes.

tested, as illustrated in FIG. 2.3. A sensible procedure would be to choose three classes of outcomes: Outcomes would be assigned as follows: to class 1, if they contained more than k heads; to class 2, if they contained more than k tails; and otherwise to class 3. Then for some particular choice of k, we could compute probabilities to be assigned to each of the three classes. The value of k, our decision criterion, would be chosen so that the probability of an outcome falling in class 1 or 2 would be small, and our decision plan would be to conclude that the coin was not fair if the observed outcome fell in either class 1 or class 2.

For 10 coin tosses, there are 1024 possible outcomes, all of which have equal probabilities of 1/1024, or approximately .001. A reasonable choice of k in this example would be 2, because the probability of 9 or 10 heads and the probability of 9 or 10 tails are each equal to .01; thus, the

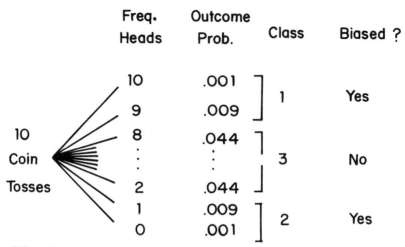

FIG. 2.3. Outcome tree for coin-tossing experiment. The possible outcomes of 10 tosses of a coin are classified into class 1, more than 8 heads; class 2, fewer than 2 heads; and class 3, all other outcomes. A result falling in class 1 or class 2 will lead to a judgment that the coin is biased.

probability that the outcome of 10 tosses falls in class 1 or class 2 is approximately .02, a small enough probability to lead one to conclude with some confidence that bias is present.

In an experiment for which a t test is planned, we go through the same procedure, and now the outcome tree comprises all possible t values that could occur. The number is infinite, but nonetheless the set of all possibilities can be partitioned just as in the case of coin tossing. We may, for example, decide to assign all outcomes with t values greater than 2.0 to class 1, all with t values less than −2.0 to class 2, and all other values to class 3, and to plan to reject a hypothesis under test if the outcome falls in class 1 or class 2.

It is a common practice among some statisticians and some social scientists to deride the use of conventional significance levels such as .05 and .01 and to recommend that investigators simply report the probabilities associated with the test statistics. In my view, some complaints about the use of conventional levels are well founded, but others are wide of the mark. I fully agree with the idea, now implemented as a requirement in some research journals, that investigators must not stop with a simple report that a result has met or failed to meet a given level of significance. Rather the value of the test statistic used and the error estimate entering into the test should always be reported, first so that readers can understand exactly how the test was carried out, and second so that other investigators can use the reported data to test hypotheses other than the one that interested the original investigator.

However, the notion that an investigator should report the exact tabled probability values associated with test statistics rather than giving a statement as to whether or not a test met a prescribed significance level is misguided. The important point here is that statistics are not just a way of garnishing research results but are applied as a basis for action. A clinical investigator testing a new treatment must at some point decide whether or not to adopt a treatment. An investigator working on a problem in basic research must decide at some point whether the data collected warrant publication. Furthermore, if statistics are to be used as a guide to action, they must be incorporated in a decision plan that prescribes which possible results of an experiment will be taken to support a particular contemplated action and which will not.

Sometimes the complaints are not about the procedure of using criterion significance levels but rather simply about the frequency with which particular levels such as .05 and .01 occur in the literature, with the suggestion that these have no theoretical basis. Here I fully agree that there is no theoretical foundation for a choice. Rather the basis is empirical. Just as we discover by experience that we require, say, 2% butterfat in our milk for palatability or 89 octane gasoline in our car for satisfactory performance, we learn in a particular line of research whether it is the .05 or .01 or some other significance level that proves satisfactory. Scanning a number of journals will readily convince the reader that modal choices of significance levels vary considerably over different research areas in psychology and social science. That observation is, I would say, not a sign of capriciousness or faddishness on the part of investigators but rather an indication that the system as a whole is working well.

The importance of adopting a specific partitioning of the outcome tree for an experiment and specifying exact criteria for rejecting a hypothesis under test is that this procedure enables the investigator both to communicate his decision plan for a study and to reason about problems and contingencies that may arise in a way that would not otherwise be possible. I will illustrate this point in terms of some common problems that face an investigator who applies statistics to aid in decisions about possible actions.

EXAMPLES OF PROBABILISTIC REASONING ABOUT DECISION PROBLEMS

Experiment-wide control of error rates

In the simplest application of statistical hypothesis testing, an investigator conducts a single experiment for the purpose of testing for the presence or absence of an effect of some one experimental variable. The purpose of applying this statistical test is to guard against a false claim, that is, a decision that an effect was present when in fact it was not. No guarantee can be offered for any one experiment, but an investigator can adopt a decision strategy such that, if he finds himself in the same situation many times, no more than some specified proportion of false claims will occur in the long run, if actually there is no effect (that is, the null hypothesis is true) in every instance. This proportion is the significance level, commonly denoted α, adopted by the investigator.

The decision plan to reject the null hypothesis if a test statistic proves to have a probability value less than or equal to α, and accept the null hypothesis otherwise, is often criticized on various grounds. One criticism is that the result of the test, when positive, says nothing about the magnitude of any effect, thus, the result of a test may be to justify the report of the presence of an effect with high confidence but with no information about the magnitude. The answer to this criticism is that it is not a good idea to meddle with a sound procedure merely because it does not achieve everything one might wish. There are good reasons to be at least as much concerned with the size as with the significance of experimental effects, and, thus, it is good procedure to accompany every report of a statistical hypothesis test with some estimate of effect size. This recommendation will receive attention repeatedly throughout the course of this book. Another criticism is that it may be rarely true in actual research situations that an experimental variable exerts no effect whatever so that a null hypothesis is strictly true; thus, significance levels hold for idealized, not for actual, research situations. The premise of that criticism is undoubtedly correct, but the implication that there is something wrong with standard hypothesis testing methods does not follow. The fact that completely true null hypotheses must be rare is recognized by the research community and implicitly taken into account in arriving at conventional significance levels that prove to be suitable guides to practice in different research areas. By adopting a definite decision plan and a specific significance level, the investigator buys a specifiable degree of protection against risk of false claims in a worst-case scenario.

The advantages of the exact reasoning that can be conducted for idealized situations becomes more sharply apparent as soon as the problem at hand becomes a bit more complicated. Consider, for example, an investigator whose study includes tests on several variables each yielding a test statistic and, thus, each with some hazard of a false claim, if the effect is absent. Given a significance level α, the probability of accepting the null hypothesis when no effect exists is $1-\alpha$ for any one test. However, if two tests are done with the null hypothesis being true in both cases, the probability of accepting the true null hypothesis twice is only $(1-\alpha)^2$, and in general, if k tests are done, the probability of accepting all k true null hypotheses is $(1-\alpha)^k$, which will become small regardless of the value chosen for α as k increases, meaning that the likelihood of making one or more false claims commensurately increases. If, for example, five tests were done with α set equal to .05, the likelihood of making one or more false claims, if the null hypotheses were true on all 5 tests, would be approximately .23.

Recognition of this relationship between the number of hypotheses tested in a situation and the likelihood of one or more false claims has led to various attempts to devise correction procedures that will maintain a desired degree of protection. The simplest of these, known as the Bonferroni correction, is derived by a simple extension of the reasoning illustrated previously. If we have set a significance level α and carry out two independent statistical tests in a situation, then the probability of at least one false claim if the null hypothesis is true is given by

$$P_2 = 1 - (1-\alpha)^2 = 2\alpha - \alpha^2 \qquad (2.1)$$

If α is equal to .05, then the right hand side of this equation becomes $(1 - .05)^2 = .0975$. We observe: If we wish the significance level of $\alpha = .05$ to hold for the whole experiment rather than just for either of the tests separately, we can approximate that result, if we divide the single test α by 2; then the righthand side of Equation 2.1 becomes .05 − $(.025)^2 = .0494$. More generally, if we do k tests, then the expression for probability of at least one error is

$$P_k = 1 - (1-\alpha)^k = k\alpha - S, \qquad (2.2)$$

where S is a collection of terms involving powers of α and has a value that is small relative to $k\alpha$. We see that to maintain a significance level α for the whole study, we should divide the single-test α by k. It is apparent also that using this correction is slightly conservative; that is, if we use α/k as the criterion significance level for each of k independent tests, then the significance level for the whole collection will be slightly smaller than α.

The Bonferroni correction is widely used, with good reason, but it should not be used blindly. For one thing, the derivation of the correction depends on the assumption that the tests conducted are independent. If several t tests are computed, each based on only the data entering into the particular comparison, then the assumption of independence is likely to be satisfied. However, if several tests are carried out on a set of data as part of an ANOVA, and all are based on the same error term, then the test statistics will be correlated, and application of the Bonferroni correction will not yield the desired result.

Use of a common error term produces positive correlation among the test statistics with consequences that are easy to specify qualitatively although difficult to quantify. If, for example, the tests for main effects and interactions in an ANOVA are all based on the same error term, and if we should choose the strategy of testing main effects only if the interaction proves nonsignificant, then the true significance levels for the tests of main effects will be lower than the ostensible α value. For the case of F statistics, the degree of correlation that will occur for various combinations of degree of freedom in the numerators and denominators can be computed, the overall relation being that the correlation increases with the number of degrees of freedom in the numerators and decreases with the number in the denominators. Tables published by Hurlburt and Spiegel (1976) can be helpful in estimating the degree of bias to be expected under various conditions.

Some subtle considerations concerning multiple tests conducted within a study have to do with the definition of a study and the question of whether the tests are planned or unplanned in advance. Suppose, for example, that a study includes two experiments and that each includes two t tests. Should the value of k in the Bonferroni correction be set at 2 for each of the experiments separately, or should it be set at 4 for the combination? Taking first the case of unplanned tests, I think that no general answer is possible, for it is often arbitrary whether the two parts of such a study should be labeled as two separate experiments or two parts of a single experiment. The answer in any particular case has to turn on an analysis of the combinations of possible results that would lead to publication of either experiment separately or of the combination, and what results would lead to the dismissal of the findings as nonsignificant. If either experiment would be published, if its results met a criterion significance level, then evidently the correction should be applied to the experiments separately. If they are conceptually linked so that it would make sense to report only both or neither of the experiments, then the correction should be applied to the study as a unit.

When tests are planned in advance, usually because of the bearing of the results on some scientific issue or hypothesis, then the considerations are a bit different. Here the investigator's purpose is to obtain a certain degree of protection against a false claim that the scientific hypothesis is substantiated, and it makes no obvious difference whether the individual tests come from the same experiment or several different experiments, or for that matter whether they were done at about the same time or strung out over a period of months or years. If k individual tests are conceptually related in that positive results from any of them will be taken to support a given scientific hypothesis, then the Bonferroni correction for k tests is appropriate regardless of how the tests are divided among experiments. On the other hand, if several planned tests in a single study each bear on a different scientific hypothesis, then there is no reason to apply the correction at all.

Significance levels for dependent experiments

The same kind of reasoning that yields the Bonferroni correction for familywide significance within a study is applicable to many problems concerning significance of dependent experiments. One common situation arises when an investigator carries out a pilot study and on the basis of the results decides whether to follow it up with a main experiment. For simplicity, we will assume that the two experiments of a pair involve the same number of observations; also we assume that, prior to any experiment, the investigator decides on a criterion significance level, α, such that if the test statistic (for example, t) reaches that level of significance in the case of the pilot study, the main experiment will be done, and if it is reached in the main experiment, the null hypothesis (no effect) will be rejected. In the following, the pilot and main experiments will simply be referred to as Experiment 1 and Experiment 2, respectively.

If the result of Experiment 1 is just significant at the α level, what should one expect as the most likely outcome of Experiment 2? If the null hypothesis is true, the answer is that, on the average, Experiment 2 will fall short of significance at the α level. The reason is that the outcome of Experiment 1 had to exceed the α criterion in order for Experiment 2 to be done, but the result of Experiment 2 is free to yield any possible value of the test statistic, and the obtained value is most likely to be near the mean of the distribution (zero when the null hypothesis is true) rather than beyond the α criterion. If, over a series of studies, the null hypothesis is sometimes true and sometimes false, then the regression toward zero will be attenuated, but still on the average the significance level for Experiment 2 will be short of that reached in Experiment 1. Appreciation of this principle is the reason why an investigator who would be satisfied with a certain significance level, say .05, when deciding whether a study reported by another investigator should be accepted as significant, may nonetheless choose to require a more stringent level for his own work in order to reduce the likelihood that others will fail to replicate it.

What can be said about the combined significance level of the pair of dependent experiments taken together? The critical consideration is that a decision about continuation is made on the basis of Experiment 1, with Experiment 2 being done only if the criterion level is exceeded in Experiment 1. In general, the values chosen for α in Experiment 1 and Experiment 2 may be different, say α_1 and α_2, producing the outcome tree shown in FIG. 2.4. Under these conditions, it is easy to determine the probability that the null hypothesis will be rejected, even if it is actually true. Denoting this probability by P, one can see that the probability, $1-P$, of accepting a true null hypothesis, is given by

$$1 - P = 1 - \alpha_1 + \alpha_1(1-\alpha_2) = 1-\alpha_1\alpha_2.$$

The reasoning is that the null hypothesis will be accepted if the pilot experiment fails to reach significance, which has probability $1-\alpha_1$, and also if the pilot study is significant (probability α_1), but the main experiment fails to reach its level of significance, which has probability $1-\alpha_2$. The probability of rejecting a true null hypothesis is then

$$P = \alpha_1\alpha_2.$$

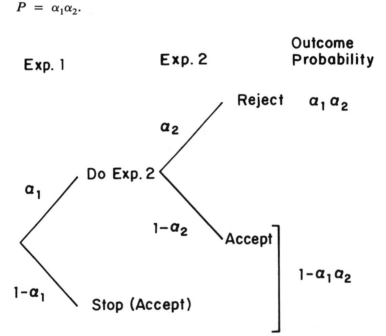

FIG. 2.4. Outcome tree for a study in which Experiment 2 is conducted only if the result of Experiment 1 (a "pilot study") meets significance level α_1. The null hypothesis is accepted if either Experiment 1 fails to reach significance level α_1, or if Experiment 2 is done and fails to reach significance level α_2.

Because P is given by the product of two probabilities, it is clear that the significance level for the combination of two experiments is much more stringent than that for either experiment alone. For example, if both α_1 and α_2 were equal to .10, P would be equal to .01, and one would be operating at the .01 significance level for the combined study.

Note that it is possible to achieve this increased sensitivity, and to know what it is, only if one follows a definite decision strategy (in this case, deciding in advance on the significance levels to be used and the decisions to be made, in case they are satisfied or not satisfied in each of the experiments). If an experimenter should simply carry out a pilot followed by a main experiment without any plan in mind and then bring us the obtained significance levels calculated for the two experiments separately, we would not be able to combine them and compute the actual significance level of the combined study.

It is important to see clearly also that the significance level $\alpha_1 \alpha_2$ is attained only if the experimenter takes the result of a single pilot study as the basis for stopping or continuing with the main experiment. Suppose that instead the experimenter allows himself two chances. That is, if a first pilot study proves negative, he conducts a second with variations in procedure and the plan of giving up the project only if the second pilot also turns out insignificant; he continues with the main experiment if either pilot proves significant at a level α_1. Following the same reasoning as before, we lay out the outcome tree for the combined study as in FIG. 2.5 and by adding the appropriate terms find that the probability of accepting the null hypothesis, if it is actually true, is given by

$$1 - P = (1 - \alpha_1)^2 + [1 - (1 - \alpha_1)^2] \, (1 - \alpha_2)$$

and the probability of rejecting the null hypothesis, if it is true, by

$$
\begin{aligned}
P &= \alpha_1 \alpha_2 + (1 - \alpha_1)\alpha_1 \alpha_2 \\
&= (2\alpha_1 - \alpha_1^2)\alpha_2 \\
&= [1 - (1 - \alpha_1)^2]\alpha_2.
\end{aligned}
$$

It is easy to see that the quantity in brackets is greater than α_1, and, therefore, the significance level in this case is less stringent than that for the simpler case of just a single pilot experiment followed by a main experiment. The investigator has gained some protection against rejecting an actually true null hypothesis with this scheme of two pilot experiments followed under some circumstances by a main experiment over the situation that would exist, if only a single experiment were done,

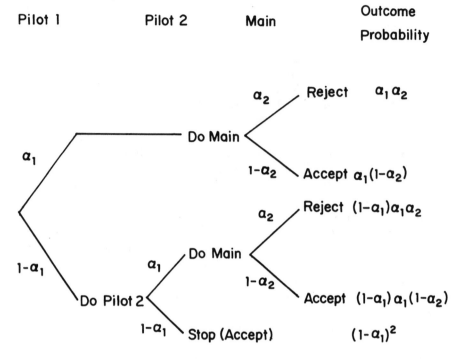

FIG. 2.5. Outcome tree for a study conducted with the decision strategy that a nonsignificant outcome of Pilot Experiment 1 leads to conducting Pilot Experiment 2: the Main Experiment is done if either Pilot 1 or Pilot 2 is significant at the α_1 level. The null hypothesis is accepted if Pilot 2 fails to meet the α_1 level, or if the Main Experiment is done and fails to meet the α_2 level.

but not as much as in the scheme of a single pilot followed by a main experiment. The argument can easily be extended. If, in the extreme case, a tireless experimenter continued doing pilot experiments till one proved significant at level α_1, then the pilot results would add nothing to the overall significance of the study, which would be simply α_2, the level of the main experiment alone.

It cannot be too strongly emphasized that the reasoning and the conclusions given here apply only if a decision is made on the basis of Experiment 1 under a decision strategy such that, if the outcome fails to meet a prescribed significance level, Experiment 2 will not be conducted. If one is interested in the combined significance of experiments that are independent in the sense that the decision on one is entirely independent of the results of the other, then different considerations apply.

Although I do not have a formal proof of the assertion, I think it is clear that for dependent sequences of experiments of the kinds considered previously, once the main experiment has been done, there is nothing to be gained by trying somehow to pool the results of the pilot and main experiments and obtain a single significance value based on the combined data. In each case, the information obtained from Experiment 1 has been "used up," in a manner of speaking, when the decision is made to go on from a pilot experiment to a main experiment, and there is no "left over" information from Experiment 1 that can be pooled with that of Experiment 2 to obtain a significance level better than that calculated by the reasoning given previously.

Some of the same issues arise when an investigator becomes interested in an already published experiment and decides to attempt a replication. However, it is harder to obtain definite answers, because the investigators responsible for the published experiment and the replication generally are not operating under a single, well-defined decision strategy. The results given above for pilot/main experiments would apply rigorously, if, in a rather idealized case, the original investigator had the following strategy: (a) Do an experiment, and if it fails to meet criterion α_1, accept the null hypothesis; (b) if it meets the criterion, publish the study, but consider the conclusion tentative until someone reports a replication; (c) then accept the results only if the replication also meets the criterion.

It is possible that in some areas the scientific community follows a practice of accepting a result only if an originally published study is followed by a successful replication. To the extent that this tacit decision strategy is actually followed, the principles given for pilot/main experiments are applicable—but only if all attempted replications are published regardless of outcome. If failures to replicate are not always reported, then estimated significance levels will be spuriously strict. Finally, as with the pilot/main sequence, if we are simply presented with the obtained statistics of a published experiment and a replication in a case where knowledge of the first result could have influenced the decision to do the second experiment, we have no way of making any firm estimate of the significance of the combined result. Depending on the actual situation, significance could at best be as high as that of two independent experiments yielding the same statistics; at worst, the significance might not be appreciably better than that of either experiment alone. The outcome turns on the decision strategies actually followed and the information that influences the decisions made at each step.

3 Basic Concepts

SAMPLES, POPULATIONS, AND MODELS

We use models to help us reason effectively about problem situations. For a simple initial illustration, suppose that we plan to carry out some studies of concept learning and as a first step need to find out whether a significant amount of learning occurs under the experimental conditions we plan to use. Thus, we start with a pilot experiment in which six subjects are given training in a categorization task for 100 trials. The data in terms of percentage of correct categorization over the last 25 trials are 60, 57, 61, 70, 49, and 63, with a mean of 60. The mean, and in fact all but one of the individual scores, exceeds the chance level of 50% correct; therefore, we have reason to think that an appreciable amount of learning has occurred.

We note, however, that the scores vary over a considerable range. Can we be confident that other groups of subjects given the same training would similarly exceed chance performance? To enable some definite answer to this question, we have to make some assumptions about what is going on in the situation. A set that will suffice is the following: First, we assume that the differences among scores are due solely to random error (the term *error* possibly including such factors as individual differences in ability among subjects as well as experimental error), and if we could obtain enough scores, the distribution of the whole population could be described by a normal (or Gaussian) curve around a mean value determined by our experimental conditions. We have no way of knowing the value of this true (or population) mean, but our best guess on the information at hand is the mean of our sample. Neither can we know the standard deviation of the hypothesized population of scores, but again we can derive an estimate from our sample, and it proves to be 6.93.

One more step will put us in a position to make a statement with a basis in probability theory about the significance of our pilot result. This step is to divide our estimate of the population standard deviation by the square root of the sample size ($\sqrt{6} = 2.45$), to obtain an estimate of 2.83 for the standard deviation (termed the *standard error* of the mean) of the distribution of sample means that would result, if we repeated the experiment many times with different samples of six subjects. Now we can test the hypothesis that the mean of the population of scores obtainable under our experimental conditions is greater than chance by considering the ratio of the difference between the sample mean and chance to the standard error, that is,

$$\frac{60 - 50}{2.83} = 3.53.$$

From elementary statistics, we recognize this ratio as an instance of the *t* statistic, which has the enormously useful property that, if the assumptions made are true, its probability distribution is known. Looking up the obtained value in a table of the *t* distribution, we find that, if the assumptions about error were true and the population mean were actually equal to the chance level of 50, a value of *t* as large as that observed would be a quite unlikely event (having a probability smaller than .02), a result allowing us to conclude with some confidence that learning did occur.

Although this illustration may seem merely to review very informally some familiar elementary statistics, it nonetheless points up some salient aspects of the approach to statistics in research that we will follow throughout the volume: (a) We were able to progress toward an answer to a question of interest only by shifting our focus from a sample of data actually obtained to a model, that is, a set of assumptions about the factors that gave rise to the observed data; (b) These assumptions amount to a description of an idealized picture of the situation studied; this picture may seem unrealistically simplified, but it has the advantage of enabling us to obtain a definite answer to the question of interest. The answer will be strictly true only for the idealized situation, but we proceed on the basis of a vast amount of experience in science indicating that definite answers gained by the use of simplified models are often better guides to action than answers that are vague or of unknown precision. Further, it often proves a good strategy to begin the analysis of a situation in terms of an extremely simple model, then to remove simplifying assumptions one at a time and at each step examine the effect of the relaxation. This strategy will be illustrated later in this chapter in connection with a more systematic discussion of assumptions about experimental error.

Before proceeding, it will be useful to clarify the meaning of the concepts of *sample* and *population*, used in the illustration without formal definition. There is no problem with the notion of a sample — the set of scores actually obtained in a study. From elementary statistics, we know that some salient properties of a sample are captured by the mean and standard deviation. For these, we will use the following notation. For a sample of scores denoted Y_i, $i = 1, 2, \ldots N$, the sample mean will be denoted

$$\overline{Y} = \frac{1}{N} \Sigma Y_i$$

and the standard deviation will be denoted *SD*, where

$$SD = \frac{1}{N} \Sigma (Y_i - \overline{Y})^2.$$

Population is a more sophisticated concept. Occasionally the meaning is literal, as in the case of the population of voters from which a sample is drawn for an opinion survey. However, more often the meaning is not literal, there being no identifiable population actually being sampled in a study. In general, the notion of a population always depends on the more basic concept of replication. Statistics are applicable to situations that are replicable, meaning repeatable in a particular sense. A replication of an experiment is a repetition with all identifiable causal factors that might affect scores either held constant or randomly varied. A replication of the pilot experiment described previously, for example, would be a repetition with the same procedures and the same number of trials, but a new sample of six subjects drawn from the same source as that of the first experiment. Here population refers to people who resemble the original subjects in all respects considered relevant (which might include sex, age, educational level, relevant prior experience).

However, the term population need not refer to a population of subjects. Consider a study involving only one subject (for example, an individual with a rare form of color blindness) with the experiment consisting of determining the accuracy of discrimination among a set of colored stimuli from a series of 100 observations. Here a replication would consist simply of another series of 100 observations on the same subject with the same stimuli. Now *population* refers to the set of all observations that could be obtained for this subject under the given conditions. In both cases, when a model is constructed for the situation, the population is assumed to be infinite, although in actuality only a finite number of relevant subjects would exist in the first case, and only a finite number of observations could be obtained from the single subject in the second case.

It is important to be clear that it is not necessary that replication of a situation can be accomplished in practice, only that the concept is meaningful. For example, in the second illustration, it might not be possible to obtain repeated sets of 100 observations on the subject under constant conditions because of variations in the internal state of the subject. Thus, in constructing a model for the situation, the term *population* would refer to the imaginary collection of observations that could be obtained on the subject, if an indefinite number of repetitions without changes in the experimental conditions were actually possible.

Our notation for statistics of populations will follow the common convention of using μ for the population mean and σ^2 for the population variance.

In dealing with relationships between samples and populations, we shall frequently need to make use of the notion of an *expectation*, that is the population mean of a sample statistic, denoted by $E()$. Sometimes a population statistic is simply the expected value of the corresponding sample statistic. For example, $\mu = E(\overline{Y})$. The population variance, σ^2, is not equal to the expectation of the squared sample standard deviation, but, as will be demonstrated in the following section, it is possible to find another sample statistic whose expectation is equal to σ^2.

We will not give a formal mathematical definition of an expectation, but we will make frequent use of the following properties:

1. If X is any random variable (for example, a score arising from an experimental observation) or a function (for example, a mean) of a random variable, and c is a constant, then

$$E(cX) = cE(X).$$

2. If X_1 and X_2 are any two random variables or functions of random variables, then

$$E(X_1 + X_2) = E(X_1) + E(X_2).$$

3. More generally, we can express the expectation of any linear combination of random variables in the form

$$E(\Sigma_i c_i X_i) = \Sigma_i c_i E(X_i).$$

In a frequent application, c_i is the number of cases in a sample and X_i the sample mean ($c_i = n_i$ and $X_i = \overline{Y}_i$ in the usual notation), so we can write

$$E(\Sigma_i n_i \overline{Y}_i) = \Sigma_i n_i E(\overline{Y}_i) = \Sigma_i n_i \mu_i.$$

The remaining population statistic that will be constantly used is the covariance, a measure of association or covariation between two quantities. If X and Y are scores drawn from two populations, the covariance of X and Y is defined as

$$Cov(XY) = E[(X - \mu_X)(Y - \mu_Y)].$$

The covariance has properties similar to those of a correlation coefficient except that its value is not constrained between -1 and $+1$. However, the covariance divided by $\sigma_X \sigma_Y$ is the Pearson coefficient of correlation.

With this introduction, we turn now to the first stage in becoming acquainted with the theoretical framework that will organize all of our treatments of specific topics. It will be seen that the minimodel sketched previously for illustrative purposes is just the most stripped-down, special case of a general model. An important advantage of the strategy of proceeding from the simplest to more complex cases is that results we obtain in simple cases will often prove to serve as modules or building-blocks that reappear in more general models, thus, facilitating enormously the task of analyzing complex research situations.

A FIRST LOOK AT LINEAR STATISTICAL MODELS: ASSUMPTIONS ABOUT ERROR

The main purpose of the statistical methods to be studied in the remainder of the volume is to enable us to use sample data as a basis for inferences about populations. Statistics such as the mean and standard deviation of a sample describe properties of the data in a compact way, but they may also yield estimates of statistics that describe properties of populations. Estimation can only be done effectively within the framework of a model, and in the case of analysis of variance and regression, the needed framework is provided by what is called the *general linear model*. This term actually refers to a family of models, of which the simplest is associated with the equation

$$Y_i = \mu + e_i \ (i = 1, 2, \ldots, N). \tag{3.1}$$

The equation expresses symbolically the idea that any score Y_i in a sample of N all obtained under the same conditions can be represented as the sum of a constant μ, the mean of the population being sampled, and an error variable e_i that fluctuates randomly in size over the set of scores. There is more to the model than the equation, however—most importantly the properties assumed for the error variable. Two properties always assumed are as follows:

1. Errors are unbiased, that is,

$$E(e_i) = 0.$$

2. The variance of errors is constant over all conditions in an experiment, that is,

$$Var(e_i) = \sigma^2,$$

where σ^2 is the population error variance for a given design. Two additional assumptions about errors are required as a basis for most statistical inferences we will be concerned with.

3. Errors are independent, an idea that can be expressed as

$$Cov(e_i e_j) = 0$$

for all pairs of scores; that is, the *covariance* of pairs of errors is equal to 0 in the long run. Alternatively we may speak of uncorrelated errors, because the Pearson correlation coefficient for any pair of errors is by definition

$$r_{ij} = \frac{Cov(e_i e_j)}{\sigma_i \sigma_j} = \frac{Cov(e_i e_j)}{\sigma^2},$$

and obviously r_{ij} is equal to 0 whenever the covariance is 0.

4. Errors are normally distributed.

It is important to keep track of which assumptions actually enter into the derivation of any statistic or statistical test and in practical situations to look for evidence as to whether the assumptions are satisfied.

This model is, of course, too simple to take us far in actual data analysis, but it will enable us to derive some quantities that will enter as modules into much of our later work.

We will start by showing how we can use two basic statistics of samples, the mean

$$\overline{Y} = \frac{1}{N} \Sigma Y_i \tag{3.2}$$

and "sum of squares,"

$$SS = \Sigma_i (Y_i - \overline{Y})^2, \tag{3.3}$$

to estimate statistics of the population. The general procedure is to derive the expectation of a sample statistic, expressed in terms of population parameters.

To obtain the expectation of a sample mean, we start with the definition in Equation 3.2 and substitute for Y_i its equivalent in terms of the model from Equation 3.1,

$$\overline{Y} = \frac{1}{N} \Sigma Y_i = \frac{1}{N} \Sigma(\mu + e_i)$$

$$= \mu + \frac{1}{N} \Sigma e_i.$$

The expectation of μ is just μ, of course, and the expectation of Σe_i is zero, because by assumption 1, the expectation of each of the e_i is zero. Therefore,

$$E(\overline{Y}) = \mu. \tag{3.4}$$

Sample means are on the average equal to the population mean, μ: therefore, we speak of $\overline{Y}$ as an *estimator*, and in fact it is the best available estimator, of μ.

The only component of a score that varies is the error term, e_i, whose variance is σ^2 by definition; thus, we should expect the population variance of scores to be equal to σ^2, and it is easy to show that the expectation is correct. By definition,

$$\sigma_Y^2 = E\{(Y_i - \mu)^2\};$$

by substitution from Equation 3.1,

$$\sigma_Y^2 = E\{\mu + e_i - \mu)^2\} = E(e_i^2) = \sigma^2. \tag{3.5}$$

If samples of size N are drawn repeatedly, the variance of sample means, also known as the squared standard error of the mean, can be obtained by the same series of steps. We start with the definition

$$\sigma_{\overline{Y}}^2 = E\{(\overline{Y} - \mu)^2\}$$

and substitute for $\overline{Y}$ its equivalent

$$\overline{Y} = \mu + \frac{1}{N} \Sigma_i e_i,$$

obtained by averaging both sides of Equation 3.1 over the sample, then simplify the result —

$$\sigma_{\overline{Y}}^2 = E\{(\mu + \frac{1}{N} \Sigma_i e_i - \mu)^2\} = E\{\frac{1}{N^2} (\Sigma_i e_i)^2\}$$

$$= \frac{1}{N^2} E\{(e_1^2 + e_2^2 + \ldots + e_N^2 + e_1 e_2 + e_1 e_3 + \ldots)\}.$$

From the assumptions of the model, we know that $E(e_1^2) = E(e_2^2) = \ldots = E(e_N^2) = \sigma^2$. Also, each of the product terms $E(e_i e_j)^2$ is by definition the covariance of the errors — because the means of both e_i and e_j are 0, $cov(e_i e_j) = E\{(e_i - 0) (e_j - 0)\} = E(e_i e_j)$, and from the assumptions of the model, the covariance of the errors equals 0. Therefore,

$$\sigma_{\overline{Y}}^2 = \frac{1}{N^2} (N\sigma^2) = \frac{\sigma^2}{N}. \tag{3.6}$$

We see that $\sigma_{\overline{Y}}^2$ is an increasing function of σ^2 and a decreasing function of N, which seems intuitively quite reasonable. The population variance, σ^2, is unknown, but we can estimate it from the sample sum of squares. By means of a derivation closely paralleling the one just done for $\sigma_{\overline{Y}}^2$ except for algebraic details, we can show that

$$E(SS) = E\{\Sigma(Y_i - \overline{Y})^2\} = \sigma^2(N - 1). \tag{3.7}$$

If we were to divide the sum of squares by N to obtain the sample variance, we would not have a good estimator of σ^2, because its expectation would be equal to $\sigma^2(\frac{N-1}{N})$. However, if we divide the sample SS by $N-1$, the expectation of the resulting quantity, denoted S^2, is equal to σ^2, that is,

$$E(S^2) = \sigma^2. \tag{3.8}$$

Thus, we take S^2 as our best estimator of σ^2. The quantity $N-1$ is customarily referred to as the *degrees of freedom* of SS, because once the value of SS is fixed, only $N-1$ of the N components of the sum in Equation 3.7 are free to vary independently.

From Equation 3.8, it is obvious that

$$\frac{E(S^2)}{N} = \frac{\sigma^2}{N}.$$

Thus, $\frac{S^2}{N}$, often denoted by $SE_{\bar{Y}}^2$, will provide our estimator of $\sigma_{\bar{Y}}^2$.

It is important to be clear about the interpretation of σ^2 and $SE_{\bar{Y}}^2$. The value of $SE_{\bar{Y}}^2$ computed from the data of a sample is an estimate of $\sigma_{\bar{Y}}^2$, the variance of the distribution of sample means that would be obtained over a series of replications of the experiment around the true population mean. One frequently sees graphs showing sample means plotted as a function of some independent variable with a band of ± 1 or ± 2 SEs attached to each mean and with the accompanying text indicating that the standard error bands portray the expected variation of means of replications around the plotted sample means. We can easily demonstrate, however, that the variance of replication means around an observed sample mean is not, in general, equal to the variance around the population mean.

Denoting the mean of a particular sample by $\bar{Y}_0$, the mean of any replication by $\bar{Y}$, and the population mean by μ, the variance of replication means around $\bar{Y}_0$, is by definition $E(\bar{Y} - \bar{Y}_0)^2$, which can be rewritten as $E[(\bar{Y} - \mu) + (\mu - \bar{Y}_0)]^2$. A bit of straightforward algebra shows that this last expression is equal to $E(\bar{Y} - \mu)^2 + (\mu - \bar{Y}_0)^2$ and, therefore, equal to $\frac{\sigma^2}{N} + (\mu - \bar{Y}_0)^2$. Thus, it is apparent that the variance of replication means around $\bar{Y}_0$ is equal to $\frac{\sigma^2}{N}$ *if* $\bar{Y}_0$ happens to be exactly equal to μ and otherwise is larger. In fact, it is often much larger. Furthermore, because SE^2 computed from a sample is on the average equal to $\frac{\sigma^2}{N}$, it yields an underestimate of the variance of replications around the sample mean.

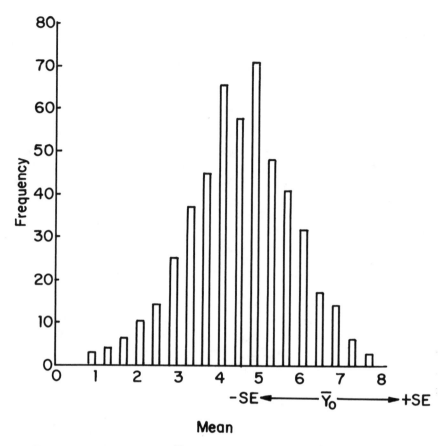

Fig. 3.1. The mean score, $\overline{Y}_0$, for a sample with an estimated standard error band together with the frequency distribution of means from 500 replications.

A typical scenario is illustrated in FIG. 3.1. A sample of five scores from a computer-generated distribution yielded the mean $\overline{Y}_0$ and estimated band of plus or minus one standard error around the mean indicated in the figure. This standard error band does not, however, provide a useful estimate of the range of scores within which the majority of replication means should be expected to fall. In fact, 500 replications were generated, and their means are seen to be distributed symmetrically around the true mean, 4.5, rather than around $\overline{Y}_0$.

BLOCKING

In a major class of research designs, we estimate experimental error from the variation among scores obtained under a particular experimental condition. Often, however, a study will give rise to several such sets of scores, and we have the problem of combining the information.

Suppose that, in testing the effect of an instructional condition, we obtain performance scores from a dozen available subjects, 8 women and 4 men. The obvious basis for estimating experimental error is S^2, computed from the sample by

$$S^2 = \frac{1}{11} \Sigma(Y_i - \overline{Y})^2 ,$$

where $\overline{Y}$ is the mean of the combined sample. However, we note that there is a difference between the scores of the 8 women and 4 men in the sample that looks too large to be due to error. We are led to suspect that the proper model is not

$$Y_i = \mu + e_i$$

for all subjects, but rather,

$$Y_W = \mu_W + e_i$$

for the women and

$$Y_M = \mu_M + e_i$$

for the men. If μ_W is not equal to μ_M, the S^2 we would obtain from the standard formula would reflect the difference between μ_W and μ_M as well as error (because each element $(Y_i - \overline{Y})^2$ in the summation that defines S^2 would reflect the difference between the subgroup mean for subject i and the grand mean as well as the deviation of Y_i from the subgroup mean).

In order to get a pure estimate of error, we could use S^2 calculated only for one of the sex groups, but then our estimate would be based on only a part of our data. A better tactic is to use the procedure known as *blocking* (attributed to R. A. Fisher). We treat our data as composed of two blocks, one block being the set of scores for women and the other the set of scores for men, and we compute the SS within each block.

For the women, we can compute the sample sum of squares

$$SS_W = \sum_1^8 (Y_W - \overline{Y}_W)^2$$

and for the men

$$SS_M = \sum_1^4 (Y_M - \overline{Y}_M)^2.$$

Applying Equation 3.7, we see that the expected values of these sums of squares are

$$E(SS_W) = (8-1)\sigma^2 = 7\sigma^2$$

and

$$E(SS_M) = (4-1)\sigma^2 = 3\sigma^2.$$

If we add both sides of these equations, we get for the expected value of the SS within blocks

$$E(SS_W) + E(SS_M) = 10\sigma^2$$

or

$$\frac{E(SS_W + SS_M)}{10} = \sigma^2.$$

Thus, we see that $(SS_W + SS_M)/10$ gives us an unbiased estimate of σ^2, *uncontaminated by the effects of any difference between* μ_W *and* μ_M. This property of blocking will be involved in virtually everything we do in treating various experimental designs.

THE IMPORTANCE OF INDEPENDENCE OF ERRORS

Before continuing on the main track, we note the effects of violations of the critically important assumption of independence of errors. A common source of nonindependence in psychological research is the use of repeated measures on the same subjects. As an example, suppose we wish to compare two sampling schemes in a study of reading speed. In one, we recruit a sample of 10 subjects and test each subject once. In the other, we recruit 5 subjects and test each subject twice. On the average, which scheme should be expected to yield the more stable data (that is, the smaller standard deviation of sample means over replications of the study)? We can prepare to answer questions of this kind by examining the consequences of relaxing the assumption of independence of errors in the derivation of the standard error of a mean.

We start with Equation 3.7 and the fact that the sample SS divided by $N-1$ is on the average equal to σ^2 and, therefore, can serve as an estimator of σ^2. Suppose that, rather than being independent, errors were positively correlated, as might occur in practice if repeated observations were made on the same subjects. Then the covariance of the e_i in the model would be some positive number rather than zero. Consequently in the derivation of the expectation of the sample SS, the terms involving expectations of the products $e_i e_j$ would not drop out. If no assumption is made about independence, then the covariance of errors in the population being sampled is given by

$$Covar(e_i e_j) = \rho \sigma^2,$$

where ρ the correlation coefficient for pairs of errors. If this general expression is used for $E(e_i e_j)$ in the derivation of the expectation of the sample SS, we obtain

$$E(SS) = (N-1)\sigma^2(1-\rho), \tag{3.9}$$

and because $S^2 = SS/(N-1)$, therefore,

$$E(S^2) = \sigma^2(1-\rho). \tag{3.10}$$

If errors are actually uncorrelated, then ρ is equal to 0, and Equation 3.9 reduces to Equation 3.7. If ρ is positive, with some value intermediate between 0 and 1, then the right side of Equation 3.9 is reduced from that of Equation 3.7, and $\frac{SS}{N-1}$ is on the average equal to a quantity smaller than σ^2; That is, S^2 underestimates σ^2.

Under the same generalized assumptions, the expression for $\sigma_{\bar{Y}}^2$ is similarly modified, taking the form

$$\sigma_{\bar{Y}}^2 = \frac{\sigma^2}{N} + \left(\frac{N-1}{N}\right)\rho\sigma^2 \tag{3.11}$$

Now, if ρ is equal to 0, Equation 3.11 reduces to Equation 3.6, but if ρ is positive, the right side of Equation 3.11 is larger than $\frac{\sigma^2}{N}$. That is, sample means vary more widely than they would, if independence were satisfied.

By rearranging the right side of Equation 3.11, we can put it in the form

$$\sigma_{\bar{Y}}^2 = \frac{\sigma^2(1-\rho)}{N} + \rho\sigma^2 \tag{3.12}$$

Now from Equation 3.10, it is apparent that S^2/N, which is an estimator of $\sigma_{\bar{Y}}^2$ in the case of independent errors, provides an estimate only of the term $\sigma^2(1 - \rho)/N$ on the right side of Equation 3.12. Therefore, if we were to use S^2/N to estimate $\sigma_{\bar{Y}}^2$ in the case of positive correlation of errors, our estimate would on the average be smaller than the actual value of $\sigma_{\bar{Y}}^2$ by the amount $\rho\sigma^2$.

These theoretical results can be illustrated in terms of the results of a sampling study in which the simple linear model was simulated in a computer program, one version having independent errors and another version correlated errors. The population parameters of the model are shown in the upper section of Table 3.1 and differ for the two versions only in that the correlation of errors was 0 for the Independence model and .50 for the Correlated Errors model. This correlation is based on the theoretical covariance of the errors on any pair of trials over replications of the experiment.

The program was used to compute statistics for 50 samples of size 5 drawn from a uniform distribution (all scores equally probable) over the integers 0-9 under each of the error assumptions, and the average means and variance estimates are shown in the lower part of Table 3.1. It will be seen that the variance estimate S^2 is considerably smaller in the correlated sampling conditions, as anticipated on the basis of Equations 3.8 and 3.10, and, therefore, the same is true for the $SE_M{}^2$ values derived from the S^2 values. However, as predicted from a comparison of Equations 3.6 and 3.11, the values of $SE_M{}^2$ computed from the actual distributions of sample means obtained in the two cases (last row of Table 3.1) differ in the opposite direction. When positive correlation of errors is present, sample means vary more widely over replications than would be anticipated on the basis of $SE_M{}^2$ estimated from sample S^2 values.

The general principle illustrated is that an increase in positive corre-

Table 3.1
Sampling with Independent versus Correlated Errors

Population Statistics		Independent	Correlated
Mean	μ	4.50	4.50
Variance	σ^2	8.25	8.25
Correlation of Errors	ρ	0	.50
Sample Statistics			
Mean	M	4.59	4.54
Est. Variance	S^2	8.58	5.73
Est. Variance of Means	$SE_M{}^2$	1.72	1.15
Observed Variance of Means		2.09	3.00

lation among errors produces a decrease in variability among scores within samples but an increase in the variability of sample means over replications of an experiment.

The effects of negatively correlated errors can readily be deduced from Equations 3.9 and 3.11, but deviations from independence in the direction of negative correlation rarely come up in practice.

In our subsequent work, we will always assume independence of errors unless some other assumption is explicitly specified.

4 Contrasts on Means

A contrast is a simple device but one with innumerable applications. Contrasts enter unobtrusively into nearly every familiar statistical procedure, ranging from a test of a mean difference to ANOVA to multivariate regression, but in most textbooks, contrasts surface to the student's attention only in the context of comparisons of means conducted after an ANOVA. Here the emphasis will be very different for two reasons. First, it is the versatility of a contrast as a basic analytical device that makes possible an integrated treatment of ANOVA and regression without the use of matrix methods. Second, as nicely pointed out by Rosenthal and Rosnow (1985), most questions of real interest to an experimenter using an ANOVA design cannot be answered by reference to the standard statistical output table of main effects and interactions but may readily be addressed by the definition of appropriate contrasts. In this chapter, the basic tools for working with contrasts are introduced, first in relation to simple comparisons of pairs of means, then in more generality.

COMPARISON BETWEEN MEANS OF INDEPENDENT SAMPLES

The expressions for the standard error of a mean derived in Chapter 3 provide the basis for inferences about population means when we are interested either in data for a single sample or in data for a cell of a more complex design, provided in the latter case that scores are independent across conditions. Now we apply the same kind of reasoning to derive standard errors for comparisons between means.

We will illustrate the formal development in terms of the data of Table 4.1, obtained from a category learning experiment in which the task was to classify symptom charts of hypothetical patients into disease categories. The scores are percentages of correct categorization responses over the learning series for four independent groups of six subjects each. Groups 1 and 2 differed only in task difficulty, the charts presented for categorization containing only six symptoms for Group 1 but eight for Group 2. Groups 3 and 4 also saw eight-symptom charts but received special instructions, those for Group 3 emphasizing the need to attend to the relationships between symptoms and categories, those for Group 4 emphasizing the value of attending to similarities between newly presented charts and charts seen on previous trials. The conceptual machinery to be developed in this chapter will enable us to test hypotheses of interest concerning differences between group means or combinations of means.

One sometimes finds the purpose of such tests stated as being to test the hypothesis that the samples of scores on which different means are based actually come from the same population. That hypothesis may reflect an investigator's purpose, but unfortunately it cannot be tested. To make a statistical test possible, we start by defining a model that allows for the experimental effects of interest either to be absent or to be present in varying degree, then choose a hypothesis that is both testable within the framework of the model and relevant to the investigator's purpose.

We consider first the simplest case of the difference between the means, $\overline{Y}_1$ and $\overline{Y}_2$, of two independent groups with equal numbers of

Table 4.1
Category Learning Data

	Group			
	1	*2*	*3*	*4*
	79	56	61	79
	80	50	56	69
	79	78	52	70
	68	61	58	62
	80	56	49	60
	91	58	55	50
Mean	79.50	59.83	55.17	65.00
SS	265.50	460.83	90.83	496.00

cases (Ns), for example, Groups 1 and 2 of Table 4.1. The model underlying our analysis is

$$Y_{ij} = \mu_j + e_{ij}, \qquad\qquad j = 1,2, \qquad\qquad (4.1)$$

representing the same model used in Chapter 3 except for the second subscript, added to identify the two groups. The variances of the errors are assumed to be equal in the populations from which the two samples of scores are drawn, whereas the population means may be either equal or unequal. We wish to test the hypothesis that $\mu_1 = \mu_2$. In terms of the model, the group means are

$$\bar{Y}_1 = \mu_1 + \bar{e}_1$$

and

$$\bar{Y}_2 = \mu_2 + \bar{e}_2$$

so the mean difference is equal to

$$\bar{d} = \bar{Y}_1 - \bar{Y}_2 = \mu_1 - \mu_2 + \bar{e}_1 - \bar{e}_2 ,$$

whose expectation is

$$E(\bar{d}) = \mu_d = \mu_1 - \mu_2 ,$$

because we know that $E(\bar{e}_1 - \bar{e}_2) = 0$.

By definition of a variance,

$$\sigma_{\bar{d}}^2 = E\{(\bar{d} - \mu_d)^2\}.$$

Substituting the expressions for $\bar{d}$ and μ_d just obtained, we have

$$\sigma_{\bar{d}}^2 = E\{(\bar{e}_1 - \bar{e}_2)^2\}$$
$$= E\{\bar{e}_1^2 + \bar{e}_2^2 - 2\bar{e}_1 \bar{e}_2\}.$$

We know from Equation 2.6 of Chapter 2 that

$$E(\bar{e}_1^2) = E(\bar{e}_2^2) = \frac{\sigma^2}{N},$$

and, because the samples are independent,

$$E(\bar{e}_1\bar{e}_2) = 0,$$

thus,

$$\sigma_d^2 = \frac{2\sigma^2}{N}.$$ (4.2)

If the numbers of cases in the two groups were unequal, say N_1 and N_2, the only change would be that

$$E(\bar{e}_1^2) = \frac{\sigma^2}{N_1} \text{ and } E(\bar{e}_2^2) = \frac{\sigma^2}{N_2}, \text{ thus,}$$

$$\sigma_d^2 = \frac{\sigma^2}{N_1} + \frac{\sigma^2}{N_2} = \sigma^2 (\frac{1}{N_1} + \frac{1}{N_2}).$$ (4.3)

The population variance, σ^2, is unknown of course, and we need an estimate of σ^2 from the data before we can carry out a significance test. If we choose to base the estimate only on the data of these two groups, then proceeding from the results obtained in Chapter 3, we can write expressions for the expected values of the sample sums of squares for the two groups —

$$E(SS_1) = (N-1)\sigma^2$$

and

$$E(SS_2) = (N-1)\sigma^2.$$

Adding the left sides of these equations yields $E(SS_1 + SS_2)$, and adding the right sides yields $2(N-1)\sigma^2$. Therefore,

$$\frac{E(SS_1 + SS_2)}{2(N-1)} = \sigma^2.$$ (4.4)

The denominator of the expression on the left side is the number of *degrees of freedom* of the pooled sample sum of squares, and the pooled sum of squares divided by its degrees of freedom is referred to as the *mean square error*, denoted *MSE*. The *MSE* is equal on the average to σ^2; therefore, we use it as our estimator of σ^2 and substitute its value for σ^2 in Equation 4.2, obtaining $\hat{\sigma}_{\bar{d}}^2 = \frac{2}{N} MSE$. (In the case of unequal

Ns, $\hat{\sigma}_{\bar{d}}^2 = (\frac{1}{N_1} + \frac{1}{N_2}) MSE$.) From Table 4.1 the MSE for the comparison

of Groups 1 and 2 is $\frac{(265.50 + 460.83)}{2(6-1)} = 72.63$, and, therefore, our

estimate of $\sigma_{\bar{d}}^2$, commonly termed the squared standard error of the mean
difference, is

$$SE_{\bar{d}}^2 = \frac{2(72.63)}{6} = 24.2,$$

and

$$SE_{\bar{d}} = 4.92.$$

The standard error of the mean difference appears as the denominator
of a t test for significance of the difference

$$t = \frac{\bar{d}}{SE_{\bar{d}}} . \tag{4.5}$$

In the present example, $t = \frac{19.67}{4.92} = 4.00$, with 10 df, significant at the
.01 level.

In the procedure just illustrated, we have obtained what we will term
a *local* error estimate, that is, an estimate based solely on the data of the
groups being compared. However, in the data of Table 4.1, obtained
from four independent groups (and generally in what will later be termed
"fixed-effects designs"), it is preferable to use a *global* estimate. The
global estimate pools the within-groups sums of squares from all groups
in the design. Based on a larger number of cases, the global estimate is
more stable than the local estimate, and if the assumption of equal
population variances across groups is satisfied, it yields a better estimate
of σ^2. For the global estimate, we extend Equation 4.4 in the obvious way
and again substitute the observed for expected within-groups sums of
squares, obtaining

$$MSE = \frac{(265.50 + 460.893 + 90.83 + 496.00)}{4(6-1)} = 65.66,$$

from which $SE_{\bar{d}}^2 = \frac{2}{6} (65.66) = 21.89$,

and $SE_{\bar{d}} = 4.19$.

The t computed from the entry of this estimate in Equation 4.5 is

$$t = \frac{19.67}{4.69} = 4.19,$$

with 20 df, significant at the .001 level. The value of $SE_{\bar{d}}$ from the global estimate of MSE is somewhat smaller than the value from the local estimate, a common although not necessary result, and with the larger number of df, the t from the global estimate reaches a considerably more stringent significance level.

Contrasts over means of independent samples

Next we wish to extend this result to the more general case of a comparison between any combinations of means. A comparison will be formally defined as a weighted sum of means, where the weights may be either positive or negative, taking the form

$$C = \sum_{j=1}^{K} \lambda_j \bar{Y}_j . \tag{4.6}$$

The λ_j (the weights) are constants with values specified by the investigator, for a comparison among K means. For reasons that will become clear as we go along, we always impose the restriction that the weights sum to zero, that is,

$$\sum_{j=1}^{K} \lambda_j = 0,$$

in which case the comparison is referred to as a *contrast*. The difference between two means is simply a contrast in which $\lambda_1 = 1$ and $\lambda_2 = -1$. Procedures for working with contrasts are developed in Rosenthal and Rosnow (1985), but our immediate concern is to show how expressions for standard errors of contrasts are obtainable in the framework of the general linear model.

As a preliminary, we note that the expectation of any contrast C is by definition

$$E(C) = E\{\sum_{1}^{K} \lambda_j \bar{Y}_j\} .$$

In terms of the model,

$$E(C) = E\{\sum_1^K \lambda_j (\mu_j + \bar{e}_j)\} ,$$

and with a little additional algebra, we can simplify this expectation to

$$E(C) = \Sigma\{\lambda_j\mu_j + \lambda_j E(\bar{e}_j)\}$$

$$= \sum_1^K \lambda_j\mu_j , \tag{4.7}$$

because $E(\bar{e}_j) = 0$.

Equation 4.7 is simply the population analog of the contrast defined for sample means in Equation 4.6. When we compute a contrast, it is usually with the purpose of testing the hypothesis that the trend represented by the sequence of λ_j values does not characterize the population means, μ_j, that is, that the λ_j and μ_j are uncorrelated. If the hypothesis is true, then

$$E(C) = E(\Sigma_j\lambda_j\mu_j) = \bar{\mu}\Sigma\lambda_j = 0.$$

To obtain the variance of the contrast, we start with the definition

$$\sigma_C^2 = Var \left(\sum_1^K \lambda_j \bar{Y}_j\right).$$

If the samples are independent with equal numbers of cases, we can continue

$$\sigma_C^2 = \sum_1^K Var (\lambda_j\bar{Y}_j) = \sum_1^K \lambda_j^2 Var (\bar{Y}_j)$$

$$= \sum_1^K \lambda_j^2 \frac{\sigma^2}{N} = \frac{\sigma^2}{N} \sum_1^K \lambda_j^2 , \tag{4.8}$$

because we already know that $Var(\bar{Y}_j) = \dfrac{\sigma^2}{N}$, where N is the number of cases in each sample. As in the special case of a difference between two means, we can obtain an estimate of σ^2 by pooling the sample sums of squares to obtain the mean square error for the contrast,

$$MSE = \frac{\overset{K}{\underset{1}{\Sigma}}SS_j}{K(n-1)} .$$

Then for purposes of a t test or the computation of confidence limits,

$$\hat{\sigma}^2_C = SE^2_C = \frac{MSE}{N} \sum_1^K \lambda_j^2 . \qquad (4.9)$$

To illustrate this development, suppose that for the data of Table 4.1, we wish to assess the effect of task difficulty by testing the significance of the difference between the mean of Group 1 and the mean of the other three groups combined. The obvious choice of weights for an appropriate contrast would be 1 for Group 1 and $-\frac{1}{3}$ for each of the other groups. However, our result will be unaffected if we multiply each of these values by 3 so as to deal with integers. The desired contrast is then

$$C = 3(79.50) - 59.83 - 55.17 - 65.00 = 58.5.$$

The variance of the contrast is, from Equation 4.8,

$$\sigma^2_C = \frac{\sigma^2}{6} (3^2 + (-1)^2 + (-1)^2 + (-1)^2) = 2\sigma^2.$$

All four groups enter into the contrast; therefore, local and global estimates of mean square error are identical and in fact equal to the global estimate obtained previously in connection with a t test between two means. Thus, we need only substitute this value, 65.66, for σ^2 in the previous equation to obtain the SE^2, or estimated variance, of the contrast.

$$\hat{\sigma}^2_C = SE^2_C = 2(65.66) = 131.22,$$

and

$$SE_C = 11.46.$$

Now we can test the hypothesis of no effect of task difficulty (that is, the population value of the contrast is equal to 0) by a t test with 20 df: We obtain $t = \frac{58.5 - 0}{11.46} = 5.11$, which is significant well beyond the .001 level.

If the means entering into a contrast are based on unequal numbers of cases, the definition of the contrast (Equation 4.6) is unchanged, and the expressions for variances require only simple modification. The expression for σ_C^2, the variance of the contrast (Equation 4.8), becomes

$$\sigma_C^2 = \sigma^2 \sum_1^K \frac{\lambda_j^2}{n_j},$$

where n_j is the number of cases entering into mean $\overline{Y}_j$, with the estimator

$$\hat{\sigma}_C^2 = SE_C^2 = MSE \sum_1^K \frac{\lambda_j^2}{n_j},$$

the MSE being obtained just as in the case of equal ns.

Contrasts over means of correlated samples

If samples are not independent, as when the same group of subjects is run under each of a set of K conditions, our results require some modification. In the repeated measures case, we might assume that the error components of all scores obtained from a given subject are intercorrelated, with population correlation coefficient ρ for any pair of errors e_{ij} e_{ij}'. The right hand side of Equation 4.8 must then be augmented by a sum of covariance terms and can be shown to be

$$\sigma_C^2 = \frac{\sigma^2}{N} (1 - \rho) \sum_1^K \lambda_j^2 . \tag{4.10}$$

If errors are positively correlated ($\rho > 0$), which would be the normal assumption in the case of repeated measures on the same subjects, then σ_C^2 will be smaller than when errors are independent.

In the simple case of a difference between two paired samples, discussed at the beginning of this chapter, we have $K = 2$, $\lambda_1 = 1$, $\lambda_2 = -1$; then Equation 4.10 reduces to

$$\sigma_C^2 = \frac{2\sigma^2}{N} (1 - \rho),$$

and if $\rho = 0$, it comes down to

$$\sigma_C^2 = \frac{2\sigma^2}{N},$$

identical to Equation 4.2.

Now we have the problem of estimating σ_C^2 from data. When contrasts are defined within ANOVA designs, there will generally be a way of obtaining a global estimate from one (or a combination) of the mean squares in the ANOVA summary table. Ways of doing this will be discussed later in connection with different types of designs. One method that will always work, however, is to compute the sample sum of squares for contrasts on individual scores from the data entering into the contrast on sample means. In a repeated measures situation for which a score Y_{ij} has been obtained for each subject in each of K conditions, we can define a contrast for each subject, the contrast for subject i being

$$C_{Y_i} = \sum_{j=1}^{K} \lambda_j Y_{ij}$$

and then compute a sum of squares, SS_{C_Y}, for the deviations of these individual subject contrasts from their mean (which is of course just the mean contrast, C, defined in Equation 4.6) —

$$SS_{C_Y} = \sum_{i=1}^{N} (C_{Y_i} - C)^2.$$

The observed SS_{C_Y} is divided by $N-1$ to yield

$$S_{C_Y}^2 = \frac{SS_{C_Y}}{N-1},$$

whose expectation is $\sigma^2(1-\rho)$, the population variance of scores in this case. The expression for $\hat{\sigma}_C^2$ then becomes

$$\hat{\sigma}_C^2 = SE_C^2 = \frac{S_{C_Y}^2}{N}. \tag{4.11}$$

This procedure can be illustrated in terms of the data in Table 4.2. These data come from a study in my laboratory in which subjects were given brief glimpses of four-letter words on a computer screen and reported the letters perceived in each word. Suppose we wish to test a

Table 4.2
Letter-Recognition Scores in Terms of Percentage Correct by Serial Position of Letter in Word

Subject	Serial Position				Contrast
	1	*2*	*3*	*4*	
1	60	80	30	80	30
2	70	20	30	70	140
3	70	50	40	80	90
4	50	40	50	50	20
5	50	50	50	60	20
6	50	60	50	80	40
Mean	58.3	50.0	41.7	70.0	56.7
Contrast wt.	1	−2	−1	2	

hypothesis, drawn from theoretical considerations, that the serial position curve should have the form of a skewed U, with the highest percentage correct at the last position, the next highest at the first position, and the lowest at the second position. An overall ANOVA yields an F of 4.59 with 3,15 df, significant at the .02 level. However, this F indicates only that the mean scores for serial positions differ significantly. To address the hypothesis of interest, we define the contrast weights shown at the bottom of Table 4.2, which line up in the hypothesized order. To the degree that this contrast departs from 0 in a positive direction, we have evidence that the means for positions depart from homogeneity in the direction of the hypothesized pattern.

The values of the contrast are given in the last column of Table 4.2, and the values in the column yield a mean of 56.7 and a sum of squared deviations from the mean (SS_{C_Y}) of 11732.2. Using this last value, we obtain the estimated variance of the contrast,

$$\frac{11732.2}{5} = 2346.2$$

from which we obtain in turn

$$SE_c^2 = \frac{2346.2}{6} = 391.0$$

and

$$SE_C = 19.8$$

With this estimate of SE_C, we can compute a t test with 5 df to test the hypothesis that the contrast is equal to 0;

$$t = \frac{56.7 - 0}{19.8} = 2.86,$$

which has a probability (one-tailed) less than .02.

Components of sums of squares

We conclude our introduction to contrasts by introducing the notion of the contribution of a contrast among means to the total sum of squares for the set of means. For any contrast C involving all or a subset of a set of K means, each based on N scores, the quantity

$$SS_C = \frac{NC^2}{\Sigma\lambda_j^2} \tag{4.12}$$

is the part, or *component*, of the total sum of squares for the K means that is contributed by the contrast C.

To illustrate this concept, consider the mean scores for Groups 2, 3, and 4 in Table 4.1. The total "sum of squares between" for these means is

$$SS_B = 290.15.$$

Now we will define two contrasts, $C_1 = (1) \times 59.83 + (0) \times 55.17 + (-1) \times 65.0 = -5.17$ and $C_2 = (-1) \times 59.83 + (2) \times 55.17 + (-1) \times 65.0 = -14.49$. For C_1, $\Sigma \lambda_j^2 = 2$, yielding

$$SS_{C_1} = 6(-5.17^2)/2 = 80.19,$$

and for C_2, $\Sigma \lambda_j^2 = 6$, yielding

$$SS_{C_2} = 6(-14.49^2)/6 = 209.96.$$

If we add SS_{C_1} and SS_{C_2} together, the result is 290.15, exactly the same as the value obtained for SS_B.

This result is not a coincidence, but neither is it completely general. A general fact is that any SS_B for a set of K means can be divided into $K - 1$ components, each associated with a contrast among some or all of the means, the sum of the components being equal to SS_B. This division can be done in more than one way, but an important restriction is that the $K - 1$ contrasts be *orthogonal*. This property does hold for SS_{C_1} and SS_{C_2} in the illustration.

If two contrasts are orthogonal, then if we multiply their λ values for each mean, the products sum to zero. In the example, we have the following:

	λ_1	λ_2	λ_3
C_1	1	0	-1
C_2	-1	2	-1
Products	-1	0	1

The sum of products obviously is equal to zero.

Testing the significance of a component is basically the same as testing the significance of a contrast. To see how to carry out a test for any contrast C in the case of independent samples, we start by obtaining an expression for the expected value of C^2. The derivation follows the same steps as the ones presented earlier for $\sigma_{\bar{Y}}^2$ and $\sigma_{\bar{a}}^2$, and yields the result

$$E(C^2) = (\sigma^2/N) \Sigma\lambda_j^2 + \mu_C^2 . \tag{4.13}$$

where

$$\mu_C = \Sigma\lambda_j\mu_j.$$

From Equation 4.12, $E(SS_C) = \dfrac{NE(C^2)}{\Sigma\lambda_j^2}$, thus, we can substitute from Equation 4.13 to obtain

$$E(SS_C) = \sigma^2 + \frac{N\mu_C^2}{\Sigma\lambda_j^2} . \tag{4.14}$$

If there are no true differences among the means, that is $\mu_C=0$, then $E(SS_C) = \sigma^2$, and we can take the value of SS_C as an estimate of σ^2. We know that the "mean square within", MS_W, for the K groups provides another, independent estimate of σ^2, because

$$E(SS_W) = E\{\sum_{i,j}(Y_{ij} - Y_j)^2\} = K(N-1)\sigma^2,$$

and

$$E(\frac{SS_W}{K(N-1)}) = E(MS_W) = \sigma^2.$$

Therefore, if the hypothesis $\mu_C = 0$ is true, the ratio of SS_C to MS_W will follow the F distribution with $1/K(N-1)$ degrees of freedom. If we set a criterion value α for our test (e.g., $\alpha = .05$ or $\alpha = .01$), then a sufficiently large value of SS_C/MS_W will have a probability less than α and will lead us to reject the hypothesis $\mu_C =0$ at the α level of significance.

In the example, MS_W, obtained from a computer ANOVA printout, is 65.66. Thus, a test of significance of the component of SS_B attributable to the contrast C_1 is

$$F = \frac{80.19}{65.66} = 1.22,$$

which is obviously insignificant. A test for C_2 yields

$$F = \frac{209.96}{65.66} = 3.20,$$

which falls short of the value (4.35) needed for significance at the .05 level with 1 and 15 *df*.

If the numbers of cases in the samples entering into a contrast are unequal, the expression for the component of SS_B attributable to a contrast C takes the form

$$SS_C = \frac{C^2}{\Sigma_j(\lambda_j^2)/n_j},$$
(4.15)

which reduces to Equation 12, if $n_1 = n_2 = \ldots = N$.

5 Testing a Statistical Hypothesis[1]

Our next task is to go through the series of steps that will take us from sample statistics to a test of a statistical hypothesis. Our immediate goal is to see clearly how various assumptions enter into the conditions for an F test.

When devising a test of a statistical hypothesis in the analysis of variance framework, the principal steps are as follows:

1. Define the model assumed to underlie the data.
2. Find a way of breaking down, or partitioning, the variation among the observed scores in such a way that one component provides an optimal estimate of the population variance, σ^2, and is distributed as χ^2.
3. Find an independent statistic of the data that is distributed as χ^2 only if the hypothesis under test is true, and take the ratio of these two quantities as a test statistic.
4. Set a criterion for rejection of the null hypothesis under test (that is, define the range of values of the test statistic that will lead to rejection).

In the ANOVA framework with a balanced design, the standard procedure is to find one statistic of the data that can be regarded as a

---

[1]For the reader generally familiar with hypothesis testing, this chapter can be omitted without loss of continuity.

pure estimate of error, that is an estimator of σ^2, regardless of the presence or absence of any of the effects under consideration, then to find another statistic that will be an alternative, independent, estimator of σ^2, if some hypothesis is true. The ratio of these statistics will have a known probability distribution, and we can determine the probability that the observed value would arise, if the hypothesis were true.

To illustrate the procedure and the underlying reasoning, we start with the simple but important problem of testing a hypothesis about a sample mean. Assume we have a sample of N scores and wish to test the hypothesis that the population mean is equal to zero. We will assume that, whether or not the hypothesis is true, it is reasonable to suppose that the population of scores sampled is described by the simple case of the linear model,

$$Y_i = \mu + e_i, \qquad i = 1, 2, \ldots, N,$$

where μ is the population mean, and the e_i are independent, normally distributed errors with variance σ^2. Given those assumptions, we know that because the error variable e_i is normally distributed, so also is the quantity

$$z_i = \frac{e_i}{\sigma},$$

which is termed a z score, defined as the difference between a variable and its mean (0 in this case) divided by its standard deviation.

Now we make use of two important theorems of statistics. The first is that the square of a normally distributed z score has the χ^2 distribution with one degree of freedom (henceforth abbreviated df), which can be expressed compactly as

$$z_i^2 = \chi_1^2 . \tag{5.1}$$

The second theorem is that independent χ^2s are additive, that is, if we are dealing with a sample of N scores generated by the linear model,

$$\frac{e_1^2}{\sigma^2} = \chi_1^2 ,$$

$$\chi_1^2 + \frac{e_2^2}{\sigma^2} = \chi_2^2 ,$$

and so on, so that in general,

$$\sum_1^N \frac{e_i^2}{\sigma^2} = \chi_N^2 . \tag{5.2}$$

An additional statistical result, proved in the Appendix, is

$$\frac{1}{\sigma^2} \sum_{i}^{N} (e_i - \bar{e})^2 = \chi^2_{N-1} . \tag{5.3}$$

Here, $\bar{e}$ denotes the mean of the e_i for the sample.

The importance of these results lies in the fact that the ratio of two independent χ^2s, each divided by its df, follows the F distribution. That is, denoting the numerator and denominator df by v_1 and v_2, respectively,

$$F_{v_1, v_2} = \frac{\chi^2_{v_1} / v_1}{\chi^2_{v_2} / v_2} . \tag{5.4}$$

By using Equations 5.1 through 5.4, we can determine when ratios of observed sums of squares can appropriately be used in F tests.

For an illustrative application, we will examine the t statistic

$$t = \frac{\bar{Y}}{SE} , \tag{5.5}$$

in the form used to test the hypothesis that the population mean is equal to 0. It will be convenient to start by squaring both sides of Equation 5.5, dividing both numerator and denominator by σ^2, and then replacing the denominator with its equivalent in terms of the sum of squares of the sample, $SE^2 = \frac{S^2}{N} = \Sigma(Y_i - \bar{Y})^2/N(N-1)$, derived in Chapter 3. We obtain

$$t^2 = \frac{\bar{Y}^2/\sigma^2}{SD^2/\sigma^2} = \frac{\bar{Y}^2/\sigma^2}{\Sigma(Y_i - \bar{Y}_i)^2/N(N-1)\sigma^2} . \tag{5.6}$$

In terms of the model,

$$\Sigma(Y_i - \bar{Y})^2 = \Sigma(e_i - \bar{e})^2,$$

so by Equation 5.3,

$$\frac{SE^2}{\sigma^2} = \chi^2_{N-1}/N(N-1) \tag{5.7}$$

and, therefore,

$$t^2 = \frac{N\bar{Y}^2/\sigma^2}{\chi^2_{N-1}/N-1} .$$

Referring again to the model, if $\mu = 0$, the numerator of this last expression is equal to

$$N\bar{e}^2/\sigma^2 \;=\; \frac{\bar{e}^2}{\sigma^2/N} \cdot$$

In this last form, we have the square of a normally distributed z score, because $\bar{e}$, the average of N normally distributed quantities, is itself normally distributed, and its variance is σ^2/N, which by Equation 5.1 is equal to χ_1^2. Thus we have shown that t^2 can be written as

$$t^2 \;=\; \frac{\chi_1^2/1}{\chi_{N-1}^2/N-1} \;,$$

that is, as the ratio of two independent χ^2s, each divided by its df, and, therefore, must follow the F distribution with $1, N-1$ df. Thus, we can write

$$t_{N-1}^2 \;=\; F_{1,N-1}.$$

Finally we note an important statistical theorem, whose proof is omitted here, to the effect that the square root of any F with 1 df in the numerator follows the t distribution, thus, justifying the assumption that the quantity on the right side of Equation 5.5 follows the t distribution.

In practice, it is not necessary for an investigator to go through a full derivation whenever an F test is contemplated. Attention to the following check points will usually suffice: (a) The analysis is based on a model in which all variability in the data is attributable to error variables[2] having the properties specified in the introduction to the general linear model in Chapter 3; (b) the numerator and denominator sums of squares of the F are statistically independent (most obviously true when one comes from variation within groups and the other from variation among group means); (c) given that the null hypothesis under test is true, the numerator and denominator of the F have identical expected values, in each case equal to the error variance.

APPENDIX

A simple proof of Equation 5.3 can be given that has some instructive features. Starting with the model defined in the text, we know from Chapter 3 that the expectation of the sum of squared deviations of the scores around the sample mean is

---

[2]Or, as will be seen in following sections, *random effects* variables with similar properties.

$$E(SS) = (N-1)\sigma^2, \tag{A1}$$

and the variance of the sample mean is

$$\sigma_M^2 = \frac{\sigma^2}{N}. \tag{A2}$$

It will be useful to note that, if we divide both sides of Equation A1 by N, we get

$$\frac{E(SS)}{N} = \sigma^2 \left(\frac{N-1}{N}\right) = \sigma^2 - \frac{\sigma^2}{N} = \sigma^2 - \sigma_M^2.$$

On rearranging this result,

$$\sigma^2 = \frac{E(SS)}{N} + \sigma_M^2, \tag{A3}$$

we see that the population variance of the scores being sampled is equal to the average variation of scores around the sample mean plus the variance of sample means around the population mean.

To carry out step 2 for the present problem, we surmise on the basis of the simple relationship expressed in Equation A3 that it will be useful to express the deviation of any score from the population mean as a sum of two components —

$$Y_i - \mu = (Y_i - \overline{Y}) + (\overline{Y} - \mu).$$

If we square both sides of this identity and sum over all of the scores in the sample, we obtain (after some algebraic manipulation) the simple result

$$\Sigma(Y_i - \mu)^2 = \Sigma(Y_i - \overline{Y})^2 + N(\overline{Y} - \mu)^2. \tag{A4}$$

The two terms on the right can be shown to be uncorrelated (statistically independent), as is intuitively apparent, because one reflects only variation within the sample and the other only the distance of the sample mean from the population mean. Finally we divide each of the terms in Equation 4 by σ^2,

$$\frac{\Sigma(Y_i - \mu)^2}{\sigma^2} = \frac{\Sigma(Y_i - \overline{Y})^2}{\sigma^2} + \frac{N(\overline{Y} - \mu)^2}{\sigma^2}. \tag{A5}$$

The importance of this result is that the quantities obtained all turn out to have known probability distributions.

To find out what these probability distributions are, we consider any one element in the sum on the left side of (5), $\dfrac{(Y_i - \mu)^2}{\sigma^2}$. This quantity is just the square of the normal deviate

$$z_i = \frac{Y_i - \mu}{\sigma},$$

and from Equation 5.2,

$$z_i^2 = \frac{\Sigma(Y_i - \mu)^2}{\sigma^2} = \chi_N^2 . \tag{A6}$$

The final step to a usable result involves getting from (A6) to an expression with similar properties that does not require our knowing the value of σ^2. Once again, we can move toward our goal by breaking something into parts. Looking back over the route to Equation A6, we note that the expression we have just found to have the χ^2 distribution with N df is the left side of Equation A5. Perhaps the terms on the right side of Equation A5 also have known distributions.

   Looking at the last term of Equation A5 with this thought in mind, we see that it could be written in the form

$$\frac{(\overline{Y} - \mu)^2}{\sigma^2/N} = \frac{(\overline{Y} - \mu)^2}{\sigma_M^2} .$$

Now it is apparent that this term is the square of the z score

$$\frac{\overline{Y} - \mu}{\sigma_M},$$

and from Equation 5.1,

$$\frac{(\overline{Y} - \mu)^2}{\sigma_M^2} = \chi_1^2 .$$

The expression on the left side of Equation A5 is equal to χ_N^2, and the second term on the right is equal to χ_1^2, and the terms on the right are statistically independent; therefore, the property of additivity enables us to conclude that the first term on the right is equal to χ_{N-1}^2. If we substitute for Y_i and $\overline{Y}$ in this term their equivalents from the model, it takes the form $\dfrac{1}{\sigma^2} \Sigma(e_i - \overline{e})^2$, which is identical to the left side of Equation 5.3.

6 Simple Analysis of Variance

The methods used to obtain the expected values of a within-group sum of squares and of the variance of a sample mean in Chapter 3 can be extended directly to derive the expected value of a sum of squares for variation among the means of any number of treatment groups. The objective is to be able to construct for any design an expected mean square (henceforth *EMS*) table, which will serve as a guide to the statistical tests that are justifiable on the basis of the model associated with the design.

To illustrate this development, we will again use the data summarized in Table 4.1, the scores being percentages of correct responses achieved by subjects in a study of category learning with 6 subjects assigned randomly to each of four groups.

A simple one-way ANOVA yields a summary table in the customary form—

Source	df	SS	MS	F	P
Treatments	3	2001	667	10	< .001
Within Groups	20	1313	66		

The model we assume for this design is

$$Y_{ij} = \mu + \alpha_j + e_{ij} , \qquad (6.1)$$

61

with $\Sigma_j \alpha_j = 0$, where α_j represents the effect of treatment j, and e_{ij} is a normally distributed error variable. In terms of the model, we can conceive each score in the data matrix in Table 4.1 as being decomposed into two parts, one component being the part predicted by the model in the absence of error and having the same value for all scores of a group, and the other component the part due to error, differing both between and within groups.

When the data are entered in SYSTAT (or a comparable program) for an ANOVA, the first step in the analysis is to compute estimates of the population parameters μ and α_j by finding the values that yield the minimum sum of squared differences between observed scores, Y_{ij}, and those predicted by the model on the assumption of no error, $\hat{Y}_{ij}$, where

$$\hat{Y}_{ij} = \hat{\mu} + \hat{\alpha}_j ,$$

the symbols with "hats" denoting estimators of the corresponding terms in Equation 6.1. The design is balanced (all groups having the same number of cases); thus, the estimators turn out to be simply

$$\hat{\mu} = \overline{Y}$$

and

$$\hat{\alpha}_j = \overline{Y}_j - \overline{Y} .$$

The predicted values are:

79.50	59.83	55.17	65.00
79.50	59.83	55.17	65.00
79.50	59.83	55.17	65.00
79.50	59.83	55.17	65.00
79.50	59.83	55.17	65.00
79.50	59.83	55.17	65.00

the columns corresponding to those of Table 4.1.

The correlation (Pearson r) between observed and predicted values is .777. The square of this quantity, customarily denoted R^2, can be shown to equal the ratio of the sum of squares between treatments (SS_B) to the total sum of squares in the ANOVA, that is,

$$R^2 = \frac{SS_B}{SS_B + SS_W} , \qquad (6.2)$$

where SS_W denotes the sum of squares within groups. In the example,

$$R^2 = \frac{2001}{2001 + 1313} = .6038 \; ,$$

which is the square of .777, and because of this equality, R^2 is often referred to as the proportion of the total variation in the data that is "accounted for" by treatment effects.

In terms of the model, expressed in Equation 6.1, the mean for a treatment group is given by

$$\overline{Y}_j = \frac{1}{N} \sum_i (\mu + \alpha_j + e_{ij})$$

$$= \mu + \alpha_j + \overline{e}_j.$$

Thus, it is obvious that the variation among the group means is due in part to any nonzero values of α_j and in part to differences among the average errors, $\overline{e}_j$, associated with the four groups. The same kind of derivation that was used to obtain the variance of a mean and the expectation of a sum of squares in Chapter 3 shows that the expected value of the sum of squared deviations of the group means around the grand mean is

$$E\{6\sum_j (Y_j - \overline{Y})^2\} = 6\sum_j \alpha_j^2 + 6(4-1)\frac{\sigma^2}{6}$$

$$= 6\sum_j \alpha_j^2 + 3\sigma^2 \; .$$

Dividing the quantity on the right by 3, the degrees of freedom between groups, we obtain the "expected mean square" for treatments,

$$E(MS_T) = 2\sum_j \alpha_j^2 + \sigma^2.$$

For the more general case of J groups of n subjects, these equations become respectively

$$E\{n\sum_j (Y_j - \overline{Y})^2\} = n \sum_j \alpha_j^2 + (J-1)\sigma^2 \tag{6.3}$$

and

$$E(MS_T) = \frac{n}{J-1} \Sigma\alpha_j^2 + \sigma^2 \; . \tag{6.4}$$

For brevity, it is customary to denote the treatment effect by θ_α^2, defined as $\theta_\alpha^2 = \frac{1}{J-1} \Sigma\alpha_j^2$, where, J is the number of treatments; thus, Equation 6.4 can be rewritten in the compact form

$$E(MS_T) = 6\theta_\alpha^2 + \sigma^2 .$$ (6.5)

Turning to the variation among scores within groups, application of Equation 3.7 of Chapter 3 yields $(6-1)\sigma^2$ for the expected sum of squares within any one group and, therefore, $4(6-1)\sigma^2 = 20\sigma^2$ for the expected total sum of squares within groups. Dividing this quantity by the degrees of freedom within groups, $4(6-1)=20$, yields σ^2 as the expectation of MS_W the "mean square within."

These results can be assembled into an expected mean square table.

Source	df	EMS
Treatments	3	$6\theta_\alpha^2 + \sigma^2$
Within Groups	20	σ^2

This simple case provides a good first illustration of the way in which *EMS* tables will serve as guides to the *F* tests that are valid in any given design. Here the expected value of MS_W is equal to σ^2, and, therefore, MS_W is an unbiased estimate of σ^2. Looking at the first row of the *EMS* table, we see that if there were no treatment effects (so that $\theta_\alpha^2=0$) the treatment mean square would also provide an unbiased estimate of σ^2. Further, these estimates are independent, because one is based on variation within groups and the other on variation between groups. We know that the ratio of these two independent estimators[1] of σ^2 follows the *F* distribution, so we can conclude that

$$F_{3,20} = \frac{MS_T}{MS_W}$$

will provide a test of the hypothesis that there are no treatment effects. The observed value of *F* allows us to reject that hypothesis.

The *EMS* table obtained for this example generalizes directly to any one-way, fixed effects design with *n* scores per condition and *J* conditions:

Source	df	EMS
Between	$J-1$	$n\theta_\alpha^2 + \sigma^2$
Within	$J(n-1)$	σ^2

---

[1]Not just any estimator will do. It is necessary that each is distributed as χ^2 (Chapter 5). In practice, one can expect that mean squares computed by well-tested programs (e.g., SYSTAT, BMDP) that use least-squares or maximum-likelihood estimation will have this property.

where

$$\theta_{\alpha}^2 = \frac{1}{J-1} \Sigma_j \alpha_j^2.$$

Denoting the sums of squares Between and Within by SS_B and SS_W, respectively, we can give a more formal statement of the condition for an F test of treatment effects. By the same reasoning illustrated in Chapter 3, we can show that SS_W/σ^2 is χ^2 distributed with $J(n-1)$ df, and if $\sigma_\alpha^2 = 0$, then SS_B/σ^2 is χ^2 distributed with $J-1$ df. Therefore, MS_B/MS_W

$$= \frac{SS_B/(J-1)}{SS_W/J(n-1)} \text{ is distributed as } F \text{ with } (J-1), J(n-1) \ df.$$

Use of *EMS* tables in resource allocation

The *EMS* table has many applications other than guiding the construction of F tests. One of these is the common problem of allocating resources, for example, experimental subjects, over treatment conditions. For a first illustration, suppose that an investigator has 30 subjects available and wishes to examine effects of levels of a treatment variable such as dosage of a drug or amount of training, a group of subjects being assigned to each level. The issue is whether to use a relatively large number of levels so as to get a detailed picture of the empirical function at the cost of a small number of subjects per group, or a smaller number of levels, sacrificing detailed information about the nature of the effect for the increase in precision associated with larger groups. We will address this issue by using the model of Equation 6.1 to estimate the effect sizes to be anticipated for these alternative allocations.

We will assume that five levels of the treatment variable are available and that they are equally spaced so that we can set the values of α_j equal to -2, -1, 0, 1, and 2. If we choose to use all five treatment levels with 6 subjects at each level, the *EMS* for treatments will be

$$\frac{1}{4}(6)\Sigma\alpha_j^2 + \sigma^2 = \frac{3}{2}(4+1+0+1+4) + \sigma^2 = 1.5(10) + \sigma^2 = 15 + \sigma^2.$$

Thus, the *EMS* table is

Source	df	EMS
Between	4	$15+\sigma^2$
Within	25	σ^2

We can conveniently take σ^2 equal to 1 (because the value will not affect inequalities in predicted effect sizes for different allocations), in which case the expected values of MS_B and MS_W respectively are 16 and 1, and the corresponding expected sums of squares 4(16) and 25. Substituting these values for SS_B and SS_W in the defining equation for R^2, Equation 6.2, yields

$$\frac{64}{64+25} = .719,$$

as our prediction of this measure of effect size for the 5-level allocation.

For the alternative allocation of 10 subjects each to levels 1, 3, and 5, a similar calculation yields an expected SS_B of $10(4+4)+2\sigma^2$ and the *EMS* table as follows:

Source	df	EMS
Between	2	$40+\sigma^2$
Within	27	σ^2

Now the expected values of SS_B and SS_T are 82 and 109, again based on $\sigma^2=1$, and the predicted value of R^2 is .752. We conclude that effect size, as indexed by R^2, would probably not differ much between the two allocations but that the expected value of MS_B would be much larger for the second allocation, which would, therefore, provide substantially greater statistical power.

An allocation problem common in experimental research arises when the investigator wishes to compare several experimental conditions with a single control condition. Suppose, for example, that in a particular study two experimental conditions, E_1 and E_2, are to be compared with a common control condition, C, and the hypothesis to be tested is that E_1 will score higher and E_2 lower than C. Two allocations of 24 available subjects are considered: 8 in each condition versus 6 in each experimental condition, and 12 in the control. Arguments can be adduced for each choice, but the problem we address is the effect of the allocation on anticipated effect size. We will assume that differences between conditions are likely to be equally spaced so that we might plausibly choose α values of 1, 0, and -1 for E_1, C, and E_2 respectively. Then the expected value of MS_B will be $8/2(1+1+0)+\sigma^2$, and the *EMS* table is as follows:

Source	df	EMS
Between	2	$8+\sigma^2$
Within	21	σ^2

Again taking $\sigma^2 = 1$, the expected sums of squares between and within are 18 and 21 respectively, yielding .462 as our prediction for R^2. In the 6,12,6 allocation, the expected SS_B is $6(1) + 12(0) + 6(1) + 2\sigma^2$, so the expected value of MS_B changes to $6 + \sigma^2$ and the predicted R^2 to .400. The equal allocation of subjects among conditions in this instance yields a larger expected MS_B and larger R^2 than the unequal allocation.

Suppose, however, that we expect both experimental conditions to differ in the same direction from the control, so that plausible α values might be 2, 1, and -3 for E_1, E_2, and C respectively. Then the *EMS* table for the 8,8,8 allocation is as follows:

Source	df	EMS
Between	2	$56 + \sigma^2$
Within	21	σ^2

which yields expected values of SS_B and SS_W of 114 and 21 respectively and predicted R^2 of .844. With the 6, 6, 12 allocation, the expected value of MS_B changes to $69 + \sigma^2$, which yields an R^2 of .870. In this case, therefore, it is the unequal allocation that yields the larger expected value of MS_B and the larger anticipated value of R^2.

The moral of this example is that one cannot specify in general the optimal allocation of a given number of subjects among the experimental and control conditions, but for any anticipated set of relationships among the experimental and control conditions, one can use expected mean squares to predict which allocation will yield the largest expected effect size and which will yield the greatest statistical power, or sensitivity.

Measuring fixed effects

ANOVA programs routinely output the value of R^2, presumably interpretable as an index of the magnitude of treatment effects. In fixed-effect designs, however, R^2 is rarely an appropriate measure of effect size. One problem is that R^2 is not an estimator of the corresponding population parameter ρ^2, unless the values of the independent variable are a random sample from a normal population, never the case in fixed-effect designs. Even more critical, the value of R^2 depends on the range and spacing of values of the independent variable and on the number of scores obtained at each level of the independent variable, as seen in the previous section.

How then can magnitudes of fixed effects be assessed? One way is to estimate population means or treatment effects (α) and set confidence limits on their values, as demonstrated in Chapter 3. In situations where this procedure does not answer the questions of primary concern, another resource is provided by regression analysis, as illustrated in the following chapter.

ONE-WAY, RANDOM EFFECTS ANOVA

In a fixed-effects situation, the investigator chooses the values of one or more factors (independent variables) and the ANOVA model enables us to derive probabilities of various events over replications of the experiment, where it is understood that the same values of the independent variables are used in all replications. Conclusions are, therefore, limited to the specific experimental conditions. In the case of the data in Table 4.1, for example, conclusions would be limited to replications of the experiment with the same materials and procedures but new random samples of subjects.

In some situations, however, the investigator does not choose specific values of independent variables or define a set of treatment procedures (as, for example, the different sets of instructions in the study represented in Table 4.1) but rather draws a number of sampling units from some population and uses these to define the "treatments" for the study. In psychological research, the sampling units are often members of some subject population or set of items (such as letters, words, nonsense syllables, test items) used as experimental materials. These units are referred to as sources of *random effects*, and the investigator's purpose in a study is to draw conclusions about a population of random effects on the basis of data obtained from a sample.

Suppose, for example, that in a personnel office it is necessary to administer an aptitude test individually to a large number of job applicants. A number of different examiners have to be used, for practical reasons, and the supervisor is concerned that individual differences between examiners might influence the scores obtained by job applicants. To investigate this possibility, a study is done in which a sample of five examiners is used, each assigned to test eight applicants. The test scores obtained are the data from which the investigator determines whether examiners in the population sampled differ in their influence on test performance.

The data obtained are entered in a one-way ANOVA program and yield the following summary table:

Source	df	SS	MS
Between examiners	4	3.48	.87
Within	35	2.84	.08
		6.32	

The next step is to define an appropriate model for the situation and determine whether the ratio of MS_B to MS_W can justifiably be interpreted as an F. The equation of the model,

$$Y_{ij} = \mu + A_j + e_{ij}, \tag{6.6}$$

looks superficially identical to Equation 6.1 for the fixed-effects model, but there is one important difference. The term α_j in Equation 6.1 represents the fixed effect of condition j and would have the same value over replications of the experiment. The term A_j in Equation 6.6, however, represents the effect of the jth examiner, who was sampled from a larger population and would be randomly replaced by some examiner (usually a different one) in any replication of the experiment. In Equation 6.1, the α_j sum to zero, but in Equation 6.6, the A_j sum to some total that varies randomly over replications of the experiment.

The assumptions about the error variable e_{ij} in Equation 6.6 are the same as for the fixed-effects model, but in addition the following are assumed:

1. The treatment effects A_j are normally distributed in the population with

$$E(A_j) = 0 \text{ and } Var(A_j) = \sigma_A^2.$$

2. The treatment effects are independent of each other and of the error variable, that is:

$$Cov(A_j A_{j'}) = 0 \text{ and } Cov(A_j e_{ij}) = 0.$$

With these assumptions, it is easy to derive expected mean squares just as was done for the fixed effects situation, and for the general case of J treatment units (examiners in the example) and n subjects per treatment unit, the result is

Source	df	EMS
Between	$J-1$	$n\sigma_A^2 + \sigma^2$
Within	$J(n-1)$	σ^2

If there are no differential treatment effects, then $\sigma_A^2 = 0$, and the mean squares Between and Within supply two independent estimates of σ^2. Thus, if the hypothesis of no effects is true, the derivations in Chapter 5 ensure that the ratio MS_B/MS_W will follow the F distribution with $J-1$ and $J(n-1)$ df.

As in the fixed-effects design, the proportion of variance accounted for by treatment effects can be measured by R^2, again defined as

$$R^2 = \frac{SS_B}{SS_B + SS_W}.$$

In the case of random effects, however, R^2 is a more useful measure of effect size, not being subject to the investigator's choice of parameter values for the independent variable. However, for historical reasons, effect size in the random effects design is more often indexed by the intraclass correlation coefficient, which in the population is defined by

$$\rho_I = \frac{\sigma_A^2}{\sigma_A^2 + \sigma^2}. \tag{6.7}$$

By reference to the EMS table, it is apparent that the constituent terms of ρ_I can be estimated by

$$\hat{\sigma}_A^2 = \frac{MS_B - MS_W}{n}$$

and

$$\hat{\sigma}^2 = MS_W.$$

Therefore, a plausible, although by no means unbiased, estimator of ρ_I is

$$\rho_I = \frac{MS_B - MS_W}{MS_B + (n-1)MS_W}. \tag{6.8}$$

From the ANOVA on the hypothetical study of five examiners given previously, both R^2 and ρ_I turn out to equal .55. However, this close correspondence of the two measures does not hold in general.

7 Regression and ANOVA in the Linear Model Framework

Although unified in modern treatments of multivariate analysis, regression and ANOVA arose in different research traditions, and the differences persist in most present day textbooks of statistics and experimental design. Analysis of covariance is usually treated as a special topic in still another chapter or omitted entirely as "too advanced." The most obvious difference between regression and ANOVA, the use of a quantitatively graded independent variable in the former but a categorical variable (or categorical "effects") in the latter, reflects the different origins. Another important difference between regression and ANOVA, the derivation of error estimates, is associated also with the different historical traditions. Although error is always formally definable in terms of differences between observed scores and those predicted from a structural model, in practice error is generally estimated differently in regression and ANOVA. In the former case, the error estimate is usually based on deviations of observed values from those predicted by the fitted regression line, whereas in the latter, error is usually estimated by deviations of observed scores from cell means, with the consequence that different error estimates may be obtained for the same set of data depending on the standpoint from which the analysis is conducted. We will see in this chapter that an examination of the underlying models points the way to an integration of regression and ANOVA that makes available all the benefits of each plus the ability to handle what were historically special topics (in particular, analysis of covariance) within a common framework.

INTRODUCTION TO SIMPLE REGRESSION

It will be convenient to begin our treatment of regression with an illustration that will follow up the preceding discussion of the problems of measuring effect size in fixed-effect designs. We suppose that two different investigators have carried out independent studies of the effect of a particular treatment on retention of learned material. The results of each experiment can be summarized in terms of percentage of material recalled at each of three retention intervals: short, medium, and long. The mean scores for independent groups of six subjects at each interval are as follows:

	Interval		
	Short	Medium	Long
Experiment 7.1	80	60	40
Experiment 7.2	70	60	50

ANOVA's on these data yield the following summary tables:

		Exp. 7.1		Exp. 7.2	
Source	df	SS	MS	SS	MS
Intervals	2	4800		1200	
Within Gr.	15	1750	116.7	1650	110.0

The observed SS yield R^2 values of .733 for Experiment 7.1 and .421 for Experiment 7.2, apparently indicating a greater effect of intervals, that is, more rapid forgetting, in Experiment 7.1. However, examination of the procedures of the two experiments reveals that the retention intervals used in Experiment 7.1 were 1, 5, and 13 days, but in Experiment 7.2, they were 1, 3, and 7 days. It may be that the difference in R^2 reflects nothing but the different choices of retention intervals. Unfortunately there is no way of correcting R^2 for the different choices of intervals, and, given only the results of the ANOVAs, there is no way to test the hypothesis that rate of forgetting was actually equal in the two studies. We can, however, achieve this objective, if we turn from ANOVA to a regression analysis.

When the ANOVAs were run on SYSTAT, retention interval (I) was declared to be categorical (Category $I=3$), and the program then computed the proper SS on the assumption that the intended model was of the form

$$Y_{ij} = \mu + \alpha_j + e_{ij}, \tag{7.1}$$

where α_j represents the effect of interval j.

To run a simple regression analysis, we use the same model specification, but omit the category statement. SYSTAT then computes SS for the regression of score on retention interval and for error on the assumption that the intended model is of the form

$$Y_{ij} = \beta_0 + \beta X_j + e_{ij}. \tag{7.2}$$

In this "regression equation," X_j denotes retention interval, β_0 is a constant, and β is the slope coefficient, which indexes the change per day in amount recalled. The output of this analysis is as follows:

		Exp. 7.1		Exp. 7.2	
Source	df	SS	MS	SS	MS
Regression	1	4628.6		1157.1	
Residual	16	1921.4	120.1	1692.9	105.8

These SS values yield R^2 values of .707 and .406 for Experiments 7.1 and 7.2, respectively. On the surface, the regression analysis yields the same conclusion of a greater effect of retention interval in Experiment 7.1 than Experiment 7.2. However, the regression output also yields estimates of the constants β_0 and β in Equation 7.2. These estimates are 80.4 and -3.21 for Experiment 7.1, and 71.8 and -3.21 for Experiment 7.2. Thus, we see that in both experiments the interval effect, indexed by the slope coefficient, has the same value—a decrease of 3.21 in mean retention score per day.

Now we can obtain our best estimate of the relation between score and retention interval in the absence of error. We need only replace the constants β_0 and β in Equation 7.2 with their estimates (and drop e_{ij}), yielding

$$\hat{Y}_{ij} = 80.4 - 3.21\, X_j$$

and

$$\hat{Y}_{ij} = 71.8 - 3.21 \, X_j$$

from which we compute theoretical values of 77.1, 64.3, and 38.6 for intervals 1, 5, and 13 in Experiment 7.1, and 68.6, 62.1, and 49.3 for intervals 1, 5, and 7 in Experiment 7.2.

The estimators of β_0 and β are derived by substituting the appropriate observed values of Y_{ij} and X_j in Equation 7.2 for each i, j combination and then finding the values of β_0 and β that minimize squared error, defined as

$$\Sigma e_{ij}^2 = \Sigma(Y_{ij} - \beta_0 - \beta X_j)^2.$$

The formulas obtained for these estimators prove to be

$$\hat{\beta}_0 = \overline{Y} - \hat{\beta}\,\overline{X} \tag{7.3}$$

and

$$\hat{\beta} = \frac{\Sigma_j \overline{Y}_j x_j}{\Sigma_j x_j^2}, \tag{7.4}$$

where $x_j = X_j - \overline{X}_j$. (Derivations are given in Howell, 1987; Winer, 1971; and many other standard texts).

A point that deserves emphasis is that $\hat{\beta}$ is simply a linear contrast on the mean scores with the λ weights in the contrast chosen to reflect the actual values of the independent variable. We can refer to $\hat{\beta}$ as a contrast, because, by definition of x_j, the terms $x_j/\Sigma x_j^2$ in Equation 7.3 sum to zero. Thus, letting

$$\lambda_j = \frac{x_j}{\Sigma x_j^2},$$

we have

$$\hat{\beta} = \Sigma_j \lambda_j \overline{Y}_j,$$

identical in form to the definition of a contrast in Chapter 4 (Equation 4.6). For Experiment 7, the values of X_j are 1, 5, and 13 with a mean equal to 6.333, so the estimate of β is

$$\hat{\beta} = \frac{80(-5.333) + 60(-1.333) + 40(6.667)}{(-5.333)^2 + (-1.333)^2 + (6.667)^2}$$
$$= -3.21,$$

in agreement with the value computed (much faster!) by SYSTAT.

The standard error of β is also obligingly output by SYSTAT. To see how it is computed, we start with the definition of the squared standard error of any contrast over a set of means, which we know (Chapter 4) to be

$$SE_C^2 = \frac{MSE}{N} \Sigma \lambda_j^2 , \tag{7.5}$$

where MSE is the appropriate error mean square, N the number of scores entering into each mean, and λ_j a contrast weight. To obtain SE^2 for β, we substitute

$$\lambda_j = \frac{x_j}{\Sigma x_j^2} .$$

into Equation 7.5, obtaining

$$SE_\beta{}^2 = \frac{MSE}{N} \Sigma_j \left[\frac{x_j}{\Sigma x_j^2} \right]^2$$

$$= \frac{MSE}{N} \frac{\Sigma x_j^2}{(\Sigma x_j^2)^2}$$

$$= \frac{MSE}{N\Sigma x_j^2} . \tag{7.6}$$

To apply this result to Experiment 7.1, we take $MSE = 120.1$ from the output of the regression analysis and obtain

$$SE_\beta^2 = \frac{120.1}{6(74.667)} = .2681.$$

Taking the square root of this result yields $SE_\beta = .518$, again in agreement with the estimate given in the SYSTAT output.

In regression analyses, just as in ANOVAs, we determine what mean square (if any) yields a valid significance test by constructing an *EMS* table. For the simple case of Experiments 7.1 and 7.2, the *EMS* tables are

	ANOVA		*Regression*	
Source	df	EMS	df	EMS
Intervals	2	$6\theta_\alpha^2 + \sigma^2$	1	$6\beta^2\Sigma x_j^2 + \sigma^2$
Errors	15	σ^2	16	σ^2

We saw in the SYSTAT output that the values of the error mean square are different for the two analyses, 116.7 and 120.1, for ANOVA and regression, respectively, in Experiment 1 and 110.0 and 105.8, respectively, in Experiment 2. However, in each case the error mean square is the appropriate denominator for an F test of the Interval, or Regression, effect (and its square root, the appropriate denominator for a t test of the hypothesis that $\hat{\beta}$ is greater than 0).

EXPANDED ANOVA

One might well ask why the error estimates in the ANOVA and the regression analysis are based on different numbers of degrees of freedom and whether there should be any difference in their interpretations. In each case, the error mean square is defined in terms of the deviations between the Y_{ij} and their predicted values, $\hat{Y}_{ij}$. In the ANOVA, the $\hat{Y}_{ij}$ are simply the group means, so the differences $Y_{ij} - \hat{Y}_{ij} = Y_{ij} - \overline{Y}_{ij}$ reflect only random variations among scores obtained under identical experimental conditions. In the regression analysis, however, the error mean square (labeled "residual" in the computer printout) is based on differences between the scores and values predicted by the regression equation. If the effects of the independent variable (retention interval in this instance) are described exactly by the population regression equation (Equation 7.2 without the error term), then the deviations of Y_{ij} from $\hat{Y}_{ij}$ reflect only the same random error factor as in the ANOVA. If, however, there are some effects of the independent variable that are not described by the linear regression function, these effects as well as those of the random factor contribute to the residual mean square in the regression analysis.

On this interpretation, it should evidently be possible to divide the Intervals mean square in the ANOVA into two components, one the linear effect, identical with the linear effect in the regression analysis, and the other a nonlinear effect. To represent this decomposition, we let

$$\alpha_j = \tau_j + \beta x_j, \tag{7.7}$$

where τ_j, a constant representing the nonlinear component of the Interval effect, has the same properties as α_j, in particular,

$$\sum_j \tau_j = 0.$$

Using this decomposition of the effect term, the model equation for a one-way ANOVA, Equation 7.1, takes the expanded form

$$Y_{ij} = \mu + \tau_j + \beta x_j + e_{ij}. \tag{7.8}$$

A simple algebraic derivation shows that the effect size term in the ANOVA *EMS* table can be similarly decomposed, viz,

$$\Sigma\alpha_j^2 = \Sigma\tau_j^2 + \beta^2\Sigma x_j^2,$$

or

$$\theta_\alpha^2 = \theta_\tau^2 + 1/2\beta^2\Sigma_j x_j^2,$$

where θ_τ^2 is defined analogously to θ_α^2, that is,

$$\theta_\tau^2 = 1/2\ \Sigma\tau_j^2.$$

Using these relations, we can break down the expected sum of squares for intervals in the ANOVA, $12\theta_\alpha^2 + 2\sigma^2$, into two components—

$$6\beta^2\Sigma_j x_j^2 + \sigma^2$$

and

$$12\theta_\tau^2 + \sigma^2.$$

Each of these components has one associated *df*, so the expanded ANOVA *EMS* table for Experiment 7.1 is as follows:

Source	df	SS	MS	EMS
Intervals				
Linear	1	4628.6	4628.6	$6\beta^2\Sigma_j x_j^2 + \sigma^2$
Nonlinear	1	171.4	171.4	$12\theta_\tau^2 + \sigma^2$
		4800		
Within	13	1750	116.7	σ^2

The linear component of the Intervals effect is identical to the linear regression effect in the regression analysis, but we see now that we can test it against the pure error estimate MS_W rather than against the residual *MS* of the regression analysis, which includes not only error but also the nonlinear part of the interval effect.

Which way of testing the linear regression effect is to be preferred? The answer is a matter of judgment. If there are strong reasons to believe that any effect of an independent variable will be purely linear, then the residual in the regression analysis reflects only error, and because it has one more df than the MS_W of the ANOVA, will provide a slightly more sensitive test. In the vast majority of research situations, however, the investigator cannot be confident in advance that the effect of an independent variable will be purely linear and must allow for the possibility of an appreciable or even large nonlinear effect. Thus, it must be the best strategy under most circumstances to employ the expanded ANOVA rather than the traditional regression approach.

When the expanded ANOVA is chosen, the contribution of linear regression to the treatment sum of squares can be calculated from Equation 4.2 of Chapter 4, with the contrast defined as $C = \Sigma \overline{Y}_j \lambda_j$ and

$$\lambda_j = \frac{x_j}{\sum\limits_{j} x_j^2} .$$

However, an easier method, if one is using a computer package like SYSTAT, is to run both the ANOVA and the Regression programs and obtain the linear component of the treatment effect in the expanded ANOVA from the output of the regression program.

TESTING A MODEL IN THE ANOVA/REGRESSION FRAMEWORK

We now have the tools to carry through the test of the theoretical model sketched in Chapter 1 in relation to FIG. 1.1. The full data that gave rise to the mean values plotted in FIG. 1.1 are given in Table 7.1[1] in terms of reaction times obtained from independent groups of five subjects at each of the five memory set sizes. Entering these data in a simple regression analysis corresponding to Equation 7.2, we obtain estimates of 396.5 and 42.5 for the constants a and b in the equation given in the middle panel of FIG. 1.1 for the straight line passing through the observed data points. The analysis program also outputs an estimate of the standard error of the slope coefficient, b, equal to 3.94; the small size of the SE compared to the value of b indicates that the true (population) slope is not far from the value estimated from the data, which incidentally is quite close to values usually obtained in experiments of this type. A t test of the

---

[1]I am using hypothetical data in this instance because, in actual research of the kind described, each subject is always tested at each memory set size, a complication that will not be taken up until Chapter 9.

Table 7.1
Data for Hypothetical Memory Search Experiment (Reaction Times for Indepen-dent Groups of 5 Subjects at 5 Set Sizes)

Memory Set Size	Scores					Mean
1	435	430	410	415	410	420
2	460	535	525	480	500	500
3	570	565	505	510	550	540
4	515	590	575	535	560	555
5	620	615	595	600	595	605
						524

observed slope coefficient against a hypothesized value of zero yields a t of 10.78, significant beyond the .001 level and leading us to reject decisively the horizontal straight line shown in the middle panel of FIG. 1.1 as a tenable alternative interpretation of the data.

To proceed to the steps associated with the bottom panel of FIG. 1.1, designed to determine whether some function other than a straight line would provide a superior interpretation of the data, we begin with an ANOVA on the data of Table 7.1, which yields the following output:

Source	df	SS	MS	F
Between Set Sizes	4	95850.0	23962.5	38.81
Within	10	12350.0	617.5	

Next we expand the Between sum of squares into a component associated with the linear regression of reaction time on set size, obtained from the regression analysis and a remainder obtained by subtraction —

Source	df	SS	MS	F
Between				
Linear	1	90312.5	90312.5	146.26
Nonlinear	3	5537.5	1845.8	2.99
	4	95850.0		

Now a test of the mean square for the linear component against the mean square within yields an F of 146.26, significant far beyond the .001 level.

A test of the nonlinear component yields an F of only 2.99, which falls slightly short of the 5% level. Thus, although the deviations of the data points from the straight line seen in the middle panel of FIG. 1.1 may look systematic to the eye, we have no statistical justification for going from the linear to any more complex function to describe the data. We conclude that, within the limits of this study, the theoretical hypothesis represented by the linear function with an upward slope is supported over any alternative model.

This procedure for testing models is by no means limited to the special cases when a model implies a linear function. If the theoretical function is polynomial in form, it can simply be substituted for the linear function in Equation 7.2, and a program such as SYSTAT will determine the best (least squares) values for the constants and compute the contribution of the regression to the between-conditions sum of squares just as in the linear case. If the function is of some other form, then the procedure involves two steps: (a) Determine the value predicted by the model for each of the observed means that enters into the ANOVA, and (b) compute a contrast on the observed means with contrast weights derived from the predicted values.

I will illustrate the general procedure in terms of an experiment on simulated medical diagnosis of the same kind discussed in connection with Table 4.1. In this case, there were 4 possible symptoms and two disease categories, A and B. Some subset of the symptoms characterized the hypothetical patient to be categorized on each trial. Thus, there were 16 different symptom patterns, and for each the true probability of disease category A in its presence can be calculated. This probability is termed the validity of the symptom pattern. One of the models under test in the study yielded the prediction that, at the asymptote of learning, subjects' probability of assigning any symptom pattern to category A should match the pattern validity.

To test the model, the mean percentage of category A judgments to each pattern was calculated for the final block of learning trials. An ANOVA yielded a highly significant F for differences among patterns (SS = 21224, $F = 16.1$, $p < .001$), indicating that it is appropriate to proceed with a test of the model. To do so, we need the contrast weight for each pattern, obtained as follows. We start with the pattern validities. For the pattern including only symptom 1, the validity (multiplied by 100 for convenience) is 67; for the pattern including only symptom 2, it is 34; for the pattern including all four symptoms, 25, and so on. The mean of all 16 validities is 30.7, so the desired contrast weights are $67 - 30.7 = 36.3$, $34 - 30.7 = 3.30$, and $25 - 30.7 = -5.7$, respectively. Using Equations 4.6 and 4.12 of Chapter 4 with the contrast weights ($\lambda_j s$) so obtained yields a value of 16315 for the component of the between-patterns SS that is attributable to the contrast. A test on this component yields an F of 191.7, significant beyond the .001 level.

Looking only at this result, we would conclude that the model is strongly supported by the data. Before drawing conclusions, however, we should complete the analysis by examining the component of the between-patterns SS that is not attributable to the contrast. Subtracting the contrast SS from the total SS between yields $21224 - 16315 = 4908$, and a test of this residual component (against the same error term used for the overall ANOVA and the test of the contrast) yields an F of 4.12, significant beyond the .01 level.

Thus, our conclusions have to be more complex than initially suggested. The model is indeed a significant predictor of the data, but although it accounts for a large part of the variation among pattern means, there is a residual part that must be attributed to some factors not taken into account in the model. In fact, in the full study from which these data came (Estes, Campbell, Hatsopoulos, & Hurwitz, 1989), it was found that another model yielded a comparably significant contrast but with the test of the residual component falling short of significance. The second model must be judged superior, because it leaves no significant component of the patterns effect unaccounted for.

The importance of doing a full analysis can hardly be overemphasized. A common practice is to test a model simply by correlating the predicted values it generates with the observed values. If that had been the procedure in this study, the correlation coefficient of $r = .96$ obtained for the first model, with r^2 indicating that 93% of the variation among pattern means was accounted for by the predicted values, might well have led the investigators to rest comfortably with that model rather than seeking a still better one.

ANALYSIS OF COVARIANCE

An occasion for considering an analysis of covariance (ANCOVA) arises when an investigator suspects that treatment effects in a set of data might have been spuriously increased or decreased owing to a confounding of levels of the treatment variable with levels of some uncontrolled independent variable. The kind of situation that may arise is nicely illustrated in a study of drug effects on rats reported by Conti and Musty (1985), cited in Howell (1987) as an illustration of ANCOVA. The study was concerned with the effects of different dosages of THC, an ingredient of marijuana, on activity level. The animals used were assigned randomly to five groups, all of which were given a pretest for activity level without the drug followed by a posttest after injections of different dosages of THC. The data shown in Table 7.2, taken from Howell (1987), represent mean activity scores in the pretests and posttests for the five treatment groups. The mean scores on the posttests appear to confirm the investigator's hypothesis that activity would first increase and then decrease with increasing drug dosage, and an ANOVA on the postscores, shown at the top of Table 7.3, yields a highly significant F for treatments. However, there is room for concern about a claim of significant treatment effects, because inspection of the pretest scores in Table 7.2 indicates that the assignment of animals to treatment groups, although random, resulted in a trend in pretest scores that quite closely mirrors that in the posttest scores. Thus, the possibility needs to be considered that the variation in posttest scores is simply a reflection of some characteristic of the animals that is measured by the pretest scores rather than actual treatment effects. To evaluate this possibility, Howell computed an ANCOVA, a summary of which is presented in the lower part of Table 7.3. The top row of the ANCOVA summary gives the sum of squares for treatments adjusted for the correlation between Y and X scores (technically the linear regression of Y on X), and it will be seen that the adjusted SS_T is markedly reduced from the values shown in the upper portion of Table 7.3. The second row of the ANCOVA summary gives the sum of squares attributable to the covariate, that is the pretest score of each animal, and the bottom row the estimate of error adjusted for the covariate effect. One would conclude from this table that the sum of squares for treatments was spuriously increased as a consequence of variation among groups in pretest level but that there was nonetheless still a significant treatment effect.

Rather than go through the traditional method of conducting an ANCOVA, I shall proceed directly to show how the values given in the lower part of Table 7.3 could be obtained by straightforward application of the ANOVA/regression model developed in the earlier portion of this

Table 7.2
Data* for Analysis of Covariance

	Treatment									
	1		*2*		*3*		*4*		*5*	
Drug dosage in μg	0		.1		.5		1		2	
Condition	Pre	Post	Pre	Post	Pre	Post	Pre	Post	Pre	Post
Mean Score	3.38	1.09	5.39	2.59	6.49	3.91	5..04	2.48	3.94	1.56

*after Howell (1987).

Table 7.3
Analysis of the Data of Table 7.2

ANOVA on Postscores (Y)			
Source	df	SS	MS	F
Treatment (T)	4	44.30	11.08	7.96
Within (W)	42	58.47	1.39	
Total	46	102.77		

ANCOVA (Postscores Adjusted for Prescores)			
	df	SS	MS	F
Adj. Treatments	4	9.22	2.31	4.70
Covariable (X)	1	38.34	38.34	78.11
Adj. Error	41	20.13	0.49	

chapter. The analysis will be conducted in the framework of the expanded ANOVA model associated with Equation 7.8 but with an additional subscript on X, yielding the new model equation

$$Y_{ij} = \mu + \tau_j + \beta X_{ij} + e_{ij}, \tag{7.9}$$

where all of the terms are defined as in Equation 7.8, except that X_{ij} now denotes the pretest score for subject i,j. The appropriate analysis for this model can now be computed by an appropriate program, for example SYSTAT with the model equation $Y = \text{constant} + T + X$, where T has been declared to be categorical with 5 levels, or by BMDP with analogous specifications, and the output yields sums of squares for effects of treatments (T), regression (X), and error exactly equal to the values shown in the lower part of Table 7.3 for adjusted treatment, covariate, and adjusted error respectively. To produce these values, the program has in effect gone through the following steps. First, the total sum of squares for the Y values, as shown in the upper part of Table 7.3, is computed. Then the parameters of model equation 7.9 are estimated by least squares and $R^2_{T,X}$, representing the fraction of the total sum of squares attributable to the treatment and regression effects in the model, is computed. The portion of the total sum of squares not so accounted for represents error, and, therefore, multiplying the total sum of squares for Y by $1 - R^2_{T,X}$, that is, computing

$$(1 - R^2_{T,X})SS_Y ,$$

yields the sum of squares labeled adjusted error in the ANCOVA summary. The adjusted treatment sum of squares is obtained by comparing the full model of Equation 7.9 with the submodel obtained by dropping the effect term, that is

$$Y_{ij} = \mu + \beta X_{ij} + e_{ij} , \tag{7.10}$$

and computing R^2_X, then multiplying the total sum of squares by the difference between R^2 for the full model and R^2 for the model lacking the effect term, that is

$$(R^2_{T,X} - R^2_X)SS_Y ,$$

yields the sum of squares given for adjusted treatments in the ANCOVA summary. Analogously the sum of squares for the covariate is obtained by applying the submodel

$$Y_{ij} = \mu + \tau_j + e_{ij} , \tag{7.11}$$

obtained by dropping the regression term from the full model, computing the R^2 for this reduced model, and then calculating the covariate sum of squares from

$$(R^2_{T,X} - R^2_T)SS_Y .$$

Thus, the computations of the various sums of squares that appear in an ANOVA output are straightforward within the ANOVA/regression framework. However, some subtleties of interpretation need attention. Unfortunately nearly all textbooks fail to specify precisely the hypotheses tested by the Fs associated with the adjusted treatment and the covariate sums of squares in the ANCOVA summary. A precise statement is that, provided that there is no interaction between the two independent variables (treatment level and prescore), then the F for adjusted treatment tests the hypothesis that all of the τ_j values in Equation 7.9 are equal, and the F for covariate effects tests the hypothesis that the slope constant, β, for the regression of Y on X is equal to 0. If there is interaction between two independent variables, then the Fs can be given no such simple interpretation, and we may well say that using an ANCOVA on the data is inappropriate.

The next question is how we can know whether or not interaction is present in a situation and, therefore, whether the analysis just described is justified. The only fully satisfactory answer would come from independent knowledge about independence or interaction of variables in the population that was sampled in the study. Such knowledge often is not available, however, and we have to make do with an estimate of interaction from the sample data. To obtain this estimate, we simply add a term for the interaction between treatment effects (τ)and the covariate (X) in the model equation, and we enter the modified equation

$$Y + \text{Constant} + T + X + T*X$$

in SYSTAT, or the equivalent instructions in another program, obtaining the following sums of squares:

Source	df	SS
T	4	.88
X	1	19.95
T*X	4	2.02
Error	37	18.11

The sums of squares in this output are computed, just as in the preceding example, by estimating the full model and then the models obtained by deleting single terms from the full model, computing R^2 for the full model and each submodel, and entering the results in the following formulas:

$$(R^2_{T,X,T*X} - R^2_{X,T*X})SS_Y = SS_T$$
$$(R^2_{T,X,T*X} - R^2_{T,T*X})SS_Y = SS_X$$
$$(R^2_{T,X,T*X} - R^2_{T,X})SS_Y = SS_{T*X}$$
$$(1 - R^2_{T,X,T*X})SS_Y = SS_{\text{Error}} .$$

The next to last of these values, SS_{T*X}, is the estimate of the interaction sum of squares. Testing the mean square for interaction so obtained against the mean square for Error yields the desired test. In practice, it is usual to set a rather lax significance level for this test, typically $\alpha = .25$, because it would be unsound practice to base conclusions on the analysis associated with Equation 7.9 if there were any material suspicion that interaction was present in the population. Regarding the other sums of squares in this last output, if interaction can be rejected, then MS_T, obtained from the row for T in the output, can be used to test the hypothesis that all of the condition means are equal in the population, and the mean square for X to test the hypothesis that the regression line for Y versus X has zero slope. If interaction cannot be rejected, then the rows for T and X in the output have no useful application.

This dissection of the machinery underlying the ANCOVA output may well seem somewhat complex, but at the least it assuredly illustrates the point that we can only understand what an analysis program does in response to an apparently simple instruction if we have a grasp of the models that guide the analysis.

8 Two-way Factorial Designs

Multiple causation is the rule in behavioral research, and consequently the greater part of research that requires more than the most elementary statistical analysis involves multiple classification. So long as designs are balanced and include only fixed effects, statistical models and the methods derived from them are direct extensions of the methodology developed in preceding chapters for one-way designs. For these cases, relevant statistical theory is thoroughly worked out; the choice of model for any particular design is usually obvious, and conditions for valid tests of hypotheses are covered by rules that the practical researcher can master and that rarely provoke disagreement among experts. However, research in psychology and social science very often requires the handling of random effects associated with the sampling of experimental subjects, interviewees, stimulus materials, experimenters, examiners, and the like; furthermore, when fixed and random effects are mixed in a multifactor design, new and difficult problems arise with respect to the choice of models, specification of conditions for valid hypothesis tests, and other major issues. Essentially all of these problems arise as soon as we move from the one-way design to a two-way classification including a fixed and a random factor, thus, my strategy will be to give a careful analysis of two-way designs with only occasional illustrations of ways of extending the treatments developed for two-way designs to higher-order classifications.

MAIN EFFECTS AND INTERACTIONS

When we move from a one-way to a two-way classification, the most obvious change in the output of an ANOVA program is the appearance of a breakdown of treatment sums of squares into main effects and their interaction. A standard ANOVA summary table in the following format has its uses:

Source	df	SS	MS	F
A				
B				
AB				
Error				

However, far too often it is transported unchanged into the pages of a research report, which then discusses only the significance of the main effect and interaction components. It is hard to overemphasize the point that very often this standard categorization does not actually fit the purposes of an investigation, with the result that the hypotheses of real interest to an investigator may never be formulated and tested.

Main effects

For a simple illustration, suppose that in a clinical study the A variable represents presence or absence of a therapeutic treatment and the B variable duration of the disorder being treated (say, short, medium, and long). A report of such a study will typically, perhaps nearly always, include a test of the A main effect as a major component, although it is most unlikely that the presence or absence of this main effect is what the investigator is interested in. A test of the A main effect is a test of the hypothesis that all of the α_i are equal to 0 in the model equation

$$Y_{ijk} = \mu + \alpha_i + \beta_j + \alpha\beta_{ij} + e_{ijk} \tag{8.1}$$

for the design. In this equation, Y_{ijk} is the score of subject k in treatment condition ij; μ is, as usual, the overall population mean; α_i and β_j denote the A and B treatment effects and $\alpha\beta_{ij}$ their interaction, and e_{ijk} is the error variable. The investigator who tests for an A main effect in this situation is most likely concerned with the hypothesis that the therapeutic effect is generally favorable, that is, that treatment has a positive effect at all levels of factor B. However, a significant A effect has no such implication; it could arise, for example, if there were a large favorable treatment effect at level 1 of the B factor, no effect at level 2, and a small negative effect at level 3. To deal with the hypothesis actually of interest, the investigator needs to test for the simple effects of A at the different levels of B, combining the results with the aid of one of the corrections for experiment-wide error rates discussed in Chapter 2, or use the error estimate provided by the ANOVA table to compute a standard error of a treatment mean and in turn confidence limits on the differences between treated and untreated groups at the various levels of factor B.

For another illustration, suppose that in an experimental study of the recognition of visually displayed words at short exposures, the A factor is the location of the stimulus word in the visual field and factor B the duration of stimulus exposure. Once recognition scores in terms of speed or accuracy have been obtained under the various combinations of conditions, an ANOVA output on the data will take the same form as the one given previously, but again the hypothesis tests provided by the summary table are likely to have little to do with the real purpose of the investigation. Suppose, for example, that five stimulus locations ranging from the far left to the far right of the visual field have been used, with stimulus words being tested in each location at short and long exposure durations. The purpose of the investigation is to test the hypothesis that recognition score is maximal at the center location and falls off symmetrically on the left and right sides as a function of distance from the center, and that similar functions hold for the short and long durations.

A test of significance of the effect of location, factor A in the summary table, would automatically be output by an ANOVA program but would be of little interest to the investigator, because it would yield no information as to whether the recognition scores vary with location in the hypothesized way. The hypothesis of real interest might well be approached by way of contrasts. Suppose, for example, that the locations had been chosen so as to be approximately equally spaced with respect to their anticipated effects. A plausible choice of contrast weights might then be $-4, 1, 6, 1, -4$, for levels 1–5 of the A factor (or of course any multiple of these weights). Now if the mean recognition scores at different locations are actually uncorrelated with these weights, the expected value of the contrast will be 0, whereas if the means fit the pattern of the contrast weights exactly, the contrast will be maximal; hence the test of the hypothesis that the contrast is equal to zero is truly germane to the investigator's purposes. To the degree that this statistical null hypothesis is rejected, the investigator's scientific hypothesis about the relation between recognition score and location is supported. Further, the contrast could be computed at each level of factor B and the difference between the two contrasts tested to get at the question of whether the form of the function relating recognition score to location is independent of exposure duration.

How to carry out these various procedures will be discussed in following sections. Here I wish only to emphasize the point that although the ANOVA table is a valuable tool, its computation is only one step in the chain of reasoning leading from collection of data to testing of hypotheses of actual interest to the investigator.

Interactions

The inclusion of interaction sums of squares in ANOVA outputs is a useful practice but one that is all too likely to lead to inappropriate interpretations and misleading discussions. It is essential to be clear that interaction is a statistical concept, not a measure of causal dependence of underlying processes. For the two-way classification, interaction refers to the term $\alpha\beta_{ij}$ in Equation 8.1, and the interaction sum of squares is obtainable as the difference between the error sum of squares for the full model in Equation 8.1 and the error sum of squares for the submodel of Equation 8.2,

$$Y_{ijk} = \mu + \alpha_i + \beta_j + e_{ijk} , \tag{8.2}$$

which lacks the interaction term. This method of estimating interaction, applicable whether designs are balanced or unbalanced, will be discussed in Chapter 10. For balanced designs, the terms μ, α_i, and β_j in Equations 8.1 and 8.2 can be estimated directly from sample means and the interaction sum of squares defined in terms of the differences between cell means and the values predicted for them from the grand and marginal means as in Equation 8.3.

$$\begin{aligned} SS_{AB} &= n\sum_{i,j} \{\overline{Y}_{ij} - [\overline{Y} + (\overline{Y}_i - \overline{Y}) + (\overline{Y}_j - \overline{Y})]\}^2 \\ &= n\sum_{i,j} (\overline{Y}_{ij} - \overline{Y}_i - \overline{Y}_j + \overline{Y})^2 . \end{aligned} \tag{8.3}$$

The appropriate use of interaction terms in ANOVAs is mainly to help the investigator answer questions about the hypotheses that can be validly tested in a given design and the appropriate choice of mean squares for valid tests. This use was illustrated in connection with the analysis of covariance in Chapter 7 and will be prominent in the interpretation of unbalanced designs in Chapter 10.

In applied research, the significance of interactions rarely has any material implication for decisions at issue. For example, in the illustration given previously of a study concerned with the effect of a therapeutic treatment, we saw that the hypothesis that the treatment is advantageous at all durations of the disorder being treated could not be evaluated by a test of the main effect of treatment/no treatment. Neither can it be evaluated by a test of interaction, for the hypothesis could be either true or false regardless of the presence or absence of interaction in the population. In theoretically based research, predictions from models are sometimes expressable in terms of presence or absence of an interaction but more often bear on the magnitudes rather than mere existence of effects and are more effectively dealt with in terms of contrasts formulated specifically for the case at hand.

Despite these reservations about simplistic uses of ANOVA outputs, the ANOVA summary table is nonetheless the starting point for analyses of factorial designs. Thus, we turn now to the technical side of dealing with these designs.

EXPECTED MEAN SQUARES IN TWO-WAY CLASSIFICATIONS

We wish to extend the concept of an *EMS* table to a two-way classification. For concreteness, the development will be illustrated by means of a hypothetical data set representing ratings, on a 0 to 10 scale, of graduate school applicants from four different schools by two raters, presented in Table 8.1. We assume that the two applications have been sampled randomly for each rater from the total set of applications from each school.

Table 8.1
Data Set for Raters-by-Schools Study*

| Raters | *Undergraduate Schools* | | | |
	1	*2*	*3*	*4*
1	7	10	6	8
	5	6	8	9
2	4	7	7	6
	6	8	4	8
Mean	5.5	7.75	6.25	7.75

*The score in each cell is a rating of a single application.

An ANOVA on these scores yields the following summary table:

Source	df	SS	MS
Raters (*R*)	1	5.063	5.063
Schools (*S*)	3	15.188	5.063
R*S	3	0.687	0.229
Within	8	21.500	2.688

The *F* values for tests of Rater and School effects have not been entered in the summary, because they depend on the investigator's assumptions in ways that we now consider.

Fixed effect designs

First, we suppose that the investigator is concerned only with these particular raters and schools and will conclude that an observed effect is significant if a test indicates that it would rarely arise by chance in replications of the study with the same raters and schools but different random samples of applications. Both raters and schools are said to be sources of *fixed effects*, because any effects would be the same in all replications. For brevity, we will denote the design as *FF* (in contrast with *RF* or *RR*, which will be used when one or both effects are regarded as random). With these assumptions, our model for the design is given by Equation 8.1, that is,

$$Y_{ijk} = \mu + \alpha_i + \beta_j + \alpha\beta_{ij} + e_{ijk},$$

where Y_{ijk} is a rating, α_i a Rater effect, β_j a School effect, $\alpha\beta_{ij}$ an interactive effect, and e_{ijk} an error variable. The model incorporates the usual assumptions about error plus the constraints

$$\sum_i \alpha_i = 0,$$

$$\sum_i \beta_j = 0,$$

$$\sum_i \alpha\beta_{ij} = 0 \text{ for all } j,$$

and

$$\sum_i \alpha\beta_{ij} = 0 \text{ for all } i.$$

The interactive effect is the difference between the population mean of cell *i,j* and the value predicted from the row and column effects, that is,

$$\alpha\beta_{ij} = \mu_{ij} - (\mu + \alpha_i + \beta_j)$$
$$= \mu_{ij} - [\mu + (\mu_i - \mu) + (\mu_j - \mu)]$$
$$= \mu_{ij} - \mu_i - \mu_j + \mu ,$$

where the μs with various subscripts denote the population cell, row, column, and grand means for the design.

Expected mean squares are derived exactly as done for one-way classifications in Chapter 6, and the result in this case is

Source	df	EMS
A (Raters)	1	$8\theta_\alpha^2 + \sigma^2$
B (Schools)	3	$4\theta_\beta^2 + \sigma^2$
A*B	3	$2\theta_{\alpha\beta}^2 + \sigma^2$
Within	8	σ^2

The symbols for effects in the table are defined analogously to σ^2 in Chapter 6,

$$\theta_\alpha^2 = \sum_i \alpha_i^2$$

$$\theta_\beta^2 = \frac{1}{3}\sum_j \beta_j^2$$

$$\theta_{\alpha\beta}^2 = \frac{1}{3}\sum_{ij} \alpha\beta_{ij}^2$$

and for any fixed effects design, regardless of the number of factors, exactly one such term appears in each row of the *EMS* table except the row for Within cells. The coefficients of the θ^2 terms can be arrived at in a common sense way. The coefficient of θ_α^2 is 8, because a particular Rater effect will contribute to all 8 of the scores produced by that rater. The coefficient of θ_β^2 is 4, because the effect associated with any particular school will contribute to all of the ratings of applicants from that school. The coefficient of $\theta_{\alpha\beta}^2$ is 2, because an interaction effect for any particular combination of rater and school will contribute to both of the ratings arising from that combination.

Following the same reasoning developed for a one-way design in Chapter 6, we observe that the mean square within (MS_W) is an unbiased estimate of σ^2. Further, if there are no Rater effects (that is, if $\theta_\alpha^2 = 0$), then the mean square for Raters (MS_A) is also an unbiased estimator of σ^2, and the two estimates are independent, because one reflects only variation between Rater means and the other only variation between scores within cells. Therefore, if there is no Rater effect, the ratio MS_A/MS_W follows the central F distribution and

$$F_{1,8} = \frac{MS_A}{MS_W} = \frac{5.063}{2.688} = 1.88$$

provides a suitable test for a possible Rater effect. Similarly MS_B/MS_W and MS_{AB}/MS_W provide suitable Fs for testing possible School and interaction effects.

We can readily generalize these results to any FF design comprising s levels of factor A and t levels of factor B, with n scores in each cell. From the model for the design, it can easily be verified that the total variation of the scores around the population mean can be expressed as

$$E(Y_{ijk} - \mu)^2 = \theta_\alpha^2 + \theta_\beta^2 + \theta_{\alpha\beta}^2 + \sigma^2 , \tag{8.4}$$

where $\theta_\alpha^2 = \dfrac{1}{s-1} \Sigma\alpha_i^2$ and so on. The first three terms on the right of this equation are fixed quantities, determined by any differences between the true means for the rows, columns, and cells of the design —μ_i, μ_j, and μ_{ij} respectively— and the overall mean, μ, so only the last term, σ^2, represents variability in the scores that would be observed from replication to replication of the experiment. To construct the EMS table, we simply enter in each row the terms from Equation 8.4 that could influence the value of the observed mean square and weight each term by the number of levels of factors not summed over in its definition:

Source	df	EMS
A	$s-1$	$nt\theta_\alpha^2 + \sigma^2$
B	$t-1$	$ns\theta_\beta^2 + \sigma^2$
AB	$(s-1)(t-1)$	$n\theta_{\alpha\beta}^2 + \sigma^2$
Within	$st(n-1)$	σ^2

In addition to showing how to form F tests for the main effects and interaction, the EMS table, together with Equation 8.4, is a guide to obtaining standard errors (that is, estimated standard deviations of sample means). If, for example, we want the standard error for the mean of any row of the design table (any level of factor A), we see from Equation 8.4 that the variance of any score is σ^2, and because there are nt scores in a column, the variance of the column mean must be $\dfrac{\sigma^2}{nt}$ (from

Equation 3.6 of Chapter 3). From the *EMS* table, we see that our estimate of σ^2 must be the MS_W, so the desired standard error is

$$SE_A^2 = \frac{MS_W}{nt} .$$

Thus, in the example of Raters and Schools, the variance of a Rater mean is given by

$$\sigma_R^2 = \frac{\sigma^2}{8} .$$

From the summary table, MS_W is equal to 2.688, so the square root of

$$SE_R^2 = \frac{MS_W}{8} = \frac{2.688}{8} = .336$$

provides the desired standard error of a Rater mean. Similarly for a School mean, we have

$$SE_S^2 = \frac{MS_W}{4} = \frac{2.688}{4} = .668.$$

The standard errors so obtained could be used to set confidence limits on the observed means or to enable tests of hypotheses that the corresponding population means have any specified values.

Using the same methods, we can construct tests of what are called *simple effects*. An example would be the effect of factor A at any one level, say level 1, of factor B. We would simply be doing a one-way ANOVA for column 1 of the design table. The sum of squares between levels of A in this column is

$$SS_{A(1)} = n\Sigma(\overline{Y}_{i1} - \overline{Y}_{-1})^2 ,$$

where $\overline{Y}_{-1}$ denotes the mean of column 1. The expected mean square for this simple effect is

$$EMS_{A(1)} = n\theta_{\alpha(1)}^2 + \sigma^2 ,$$

where

$$\theta_{\alpha(1)}^2 = \frac{1}{s-1} \Sigma_i(\alpha_i + \alpha\beta_{il})^2 .$$

This *EMS* is like the *EMS* from the A row of the *EMS* table for the full ANOVA with the factor t deleted, because the simple effect refers to only one of the t levels of factor B, and with the effect size term redefined. A derivation is given in the Appendix to this chapter.

To test the significance of this simple effect, we can use

$$F = \frac{MS_{A(1)}}{MS_W},$$

because if $\theta^2_{\alpha(1)}$ were equal to zero, the numerator and denominator would each have expected value σ^2.

If there were some reason to be doubtful about the homogeneity of variance over levels of B, we could instead form our F with the mean square in the denominator computed only for the sums of squares within cells of column 1, because

$$E(SS_{W1}) = E \{\underset{i \ k}{\Sigma\Sigma} (Y_{i1k} - \overline{Y}_{i1})^2\} = (n - 1)s\sigma^2$$

and, therefore,

$$E(MS_{W1}) = \sigma^2.$$

Random effects designs

Next we consider a similar design in which both factors A and B are viewed as sources of random effects. Continuing with the example of Raters and Schools, if we were willing to limit any conclusion drawn from the study to the particular sets of raters and schools used (that is, to draw inferences only about the frequency with which the observed results would arise by chance in replications of the study with the same raters and schools but new samples of applicants), then we could again use a fixed-effects analysis. However, if we wish to draw any more general conclusions about Rater effects or School effects, we instead base our analysis on the model

$$Y_{ijk} = \mu + A_i + B_j + AB_{ij} + e_{ijk}, \tag{8.5}$$

where the capital letters represent the effects of different raters and schools and their interaction. The standard assumption about these quantities is that A_i, B_j, and AB_{ij} have means of zero and variances of σ^2_A, σ^2_B, and σ^2_{AB} in the population from which our particular samples of raters and schools were drawn. Also it is assumed that their covariances with each other and with the error variable are all zero (that is, the effects and errors are mutually independent) and that each is normally distributed.

A logical problem that arises in connection with these definitions can be pointed out in terms of the raters and schools example. Levels of factors A and B (particular raters and schools in the example) are assumed to be sampled independently from normal distributions over replications of the study; therefore, it would be possible for a particular rater or school to appear in more than one row or column of the design table. In practice, however, one understands that the design comprises s different raters and t different schools, and the same constraint applies in almost any actual RR research one can imagine. Thus, in actuality, levels of A and B are sampled without replacement, although the model assumes sampling with replacement. If the populations are large relative to the sample sizes, the assumptions of independence and normality may be approximately satisfied, in which case the various results derived for the model can be used without modification. If not, the formulas derived for expected mean squares, variances, and so on will not be accurate. In the example, if four schools used in a study were drawn from a population of 100, we would proceed in practice as though the population were infinite. However, if the four schools were drawn from a population of only six or eight, we should change our tactics. One very tedious route would be to derive all needed results under the assumption of sampling without replacement. Other approaches that may be more attractive in practice will be illustrated in Chapter 9.

We can form an EMS table by following essentially the same procedure as for the fixed-effects analysis. As a consequence of the independence assumption, the variance of scores in the population is

$$\sigma_Y^2 = \sigma_A^2 + \sigma_B^2 + \sigma_{AB}^2 + \sigma^2, \tag{8.6}$$

each of the effects contributing its "component of variance" in a simple, additive fashion. To fill in each row of the EMS table, we refer to Equation 8.6 and enter the terms that would contribute to that mean square. In the general case, the resulting table is as follows:

Source	df	EMS
A	$s-1$	$nt\sigma_A^2 + n\sigma_{AB}^2 + \sigma^2$
B	$t-1$	$ns\sigma_B^2 + n\sigma_{AB}^2 + \sigma^2$
AB	$(s-1)(t-1)$	$n\sigma_{AB}^2 + \sigma^2$
Within	$st(n-1)$	σ^2

and in the Raters and Schools example,

Source	df	EMS
A (Raters)	1	$8\sigma_A^2 + 2\sigma_{AB}^2 + \sigma^2$
B (Schools)	3	$4\sigma_B^2 + 2\sigma_{AB}^2 + \sigma^2$
AB	3	$2\sigma_{AB}^2 + \sigma^2$
Within	8	σ^2

with the weights of the terms determined as in the fixed effects analysis.

The changes from the fixed-effects table are that the θ^2 terms are replaced by the variances of the effects, and the rows for A and B main effects contain the interaction effect.

The reason that the interaction variance is included in the *EMS* for Raters is that variation between Rater means over replications of the study will be affected not only by any Rater effects ($\sigma_A^2 > 0$) but also by variation in the interaction of Raters and Schools in different samples. If interaction is present, the magnitude of the Rater effect in any replication depends on the particular schools used in that replication, and the sample of schools varies randomly over replications, thus, producing variability in the observed Rater effect. (In contrast, in the *FF* design, the same schools are assumed to be used in all replications, so the interaction does not produce variability in the Rater effect.) Exactly the same reasoning explains why the interaction term appears also in the row of the *EMS* table for Schools.

A general rule for all designs is that the row of the EMS table for any effect includes interaction terms for all random factors that interact with it.

Inspection of the *EMS* table shows immediately that MS_A/MS_W, which provided a suitable F to test for a Rater effect in the *FF* design does not do so in the *RR* design. In the *RR* case, if there were no Rater effect ($\sigma_A^2 = 0$), the expected value of MS_A would be $\sigma_{AB}^2 + \sigma^2$, whereas the expected value of MS_W would again be σ^2. The numerator and denominator would not be estimators of the same population variance; the ratio MS_A/MS_W would not follow the central F distribution and, therefore, would not provide a test of the hypothesis $\sigma_A^2 = 0$.

Consider, however, the ratio MS_A/MS_{AB}. If there are no Rater effects, the expected value of both the numerator and the denominator will be $2\sigma_{AB}^2 + \sigma^2$. At first glance, this quantity does not look like a variance. However, both σ_{AB}^2 and σ^2 are population variances, and by the assumptions of the model, the interaction effect AB_{ij} and the error effect

e_{ijk} are independent. Therefore, the sum $\sigma^2_{AB} + \sigma^2_{AB} + \sigma^2$ is a population variance (namely the variance of $2\,AB_{ij} + e_{ijk}$). Under the hypothesis $\sigma^2_A = 0$, both MS_A and MS_{AB} are independent estimators of this population variance, and, therefore, MS_A/MS_{AB} provides a suitable F to test the hypothesis $\sigma^2_A = 0$. Exactly the same reasoning applies to the School effect, of course, so in the RR design, both of the main effects are tested against the interaction effect. The test of the interaction effect itself is unchanged from the FF design, because if $\sigma^2_{AB} = 0$, both the numerator and denominator of MS_{AB}/MS_W are unbiased estimators of σ^2.

Now that we have once gone carefully through the assumptions and reasoning underlying the use of the EMS table to guide the construction of F tests, we will shortcut the process in future applications and simply check to see whether the entries for both the numerator and denominator of a proposed F are identical if the hypothesis being tested is true.

Standard errors in RR designs

Computing the standard error of a mean or a comparison on means in a design that includes random factors requires careful attention to the inferences or decisions that may depend on the value obtained. The variance of a mean is a measure of the variability of sample means over replications of the experiment, and estimation depends, therefore, on assumptions as to which of the factors in the design are fixed and which are allowed to vary over the replications. Noting that a design is labeled RR or RF or whatever does not suffice. We will see, for example, that even when a design is labeled RR, either factor or both may be appropriately viewed as fixed in a particular derivation.

I will illustrate these points in terms of the two-way design with raters as the row factor (A) and schools as the column factor (B). In the overall analysis, both factors were viewed as random, and the purpose was to make inferences about Rater or School effects in the populations sampled. Suppose, however, that we wish to obtain the standard error of the mean for a particular rater, $\overline{Y}_{A_i}$, perhaps in order to test a hypothesis about the true (population) mean for that rater. We must start by specifying the set of possible replications of the study that would generate the population of sample means whose variance is to be derived. In this case, we wish the standard error to refer to the distribution of means obtained for row i of the design,

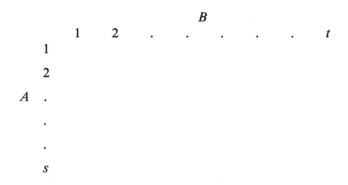

over replications in which the same rater is assigned to row i in each replication but with a new random sample of n applications from each school.

The reader may be puzzled by this statement, because in an RR design, it is assumed that the A_i and B_j (raters and schools) are drawn at random from the A and B populations. Once a study has been carried out, however, and we wish to test hypotheses involving the true mean score for a particular rater, we shift our focus to a wholly imaginary set of possible replications of the study in which the same rater is always assigned to row i but with different random samples of schools and applications. With this new focus, we can raise and answer questions about the way the mean for rater i could be expected to vary from one occasion to another as a function of experimental error and the sampling of schools and applications. Thus, I denote a rater mean by $\overline{Y}_{A_i}$, in contrast to $\overline{Y}_i$, which denotes the mean for row i viewed as a random effect so that the standard error of $\overline{Y}_i$ describes its variation over replications in each of which the sampling unit (rater) assigned to row i is drawn at random from the A population. The same comments apply, of course, to column mean $\overline{Y}_{B_j}$ and $\overline{Y}_j$.

The definition of $\overline{Y}_A$ in terms of the model,

$$\overline{Y}_{A_i} = \mu + A_i + \frac{1}{t} \sum_j B_j + \frac{1}{t} \sum_j AB_{ij} + \frac{1}{nt} \sum_{j,k} e_{ijk} , \tag{8.7}$$

makes it apparent that its variance will be influenced by variation in the sampling of schools, the interaction of different samples of schools with rater i, and sampling fluctuations. It is readily shown that these sources combine additively to yield

$$\sigma^2_{\bar{Y}_{A_i}} = \frac{1}{t} \left(\sigma^2_B + \sigma^2_{A,B} + \frac{\sigma^2}{n} \right),$$ (8.8)

where $\sigma^2_{\bar{Y}_{A_i}}$ is the desired variance, and $\sigma^2_{A,B}$ denotes the variance of the interaction variable, AB_{ij}, at the fixed level i of factor A.

This variance cannot be estimated from the mean squares in the ANOVA table for the design, because it does not appear in the *EMS* column, but it can be estimated from an analysis of the simple effect of B at level i of A. The *EMS* table for this analysis is as follows:

Source	df	MS	EMS
$B(A_i)$	$t-1$	$MS_{B(A_i)}$	$n\sigma^2_B + n\sigma^2_{AB} + \sigma^2$
$W(A_i)$	$t(n-1)$	$MS_{W(A_i)}$	σ^2

where

$$MS_{B(A_2)} = n\Sigma(\bar{Y}_{ij} - \bar{Y}_i)^2,$$

and

$$MS_{W(A_i)} = \frac{1}{n(t-1)} \Sigma (Y_{ijk} - \bar{Y}_{ij})^2.$$

The *EMS* in the first row of this table divided by nt is simply $\sigma^2_{\bar{Y}_{A_i}}$ (Equation 8.8), so the desired estimator is

$$\sigma^2_{\bar{Y}_{A_i}} = SE^2_{\bar{Y}_{A_i}} = MS_{B(A_2)} /nt.$$

The variance of a school mean takes the analogous form

$$\sigma^2_{\bar{Y}_{B_j}} = \frac{1}{s} \left(\sigma^2_A + \sigma^2_{AB_j} + \frac{\sigma^2}{n} \right),$$ (8.9)

the new term $\sigma^2_{AB_j}$ being estimable by means of an analysis of the simple effect of A at level j of B, which yields

$$SE^2_{\overline{Y}_{B_j}} = MS_{A(B_j)} / ns.$$

If we need the standard error of a cell mean (the mean for a particular rater-school combination) for this design, we have to derive the variance of scores occurring in cell ij over replications of the study in which A_i and B_j are fixed but with new random samples of applications. Under these assumptions, the only source of variation in the mean of cell ij is the sampling of applications, so the variance of the mean (from Equation 3.6 of Chapter 3) is

$$\sigma^2_{\overline{Y}_{A_iB_i}} = \frac{\sigma^2}{n} . \tag{8.10}$$

In practice, one probably needs standard errors for comparisons more often than for individual means. Suppose, for example, that in the Raters–Schools study, we wanted to test the hypothesis that two particular raters do not differ in average performance. The standard error derived previously for a single rater mean cannot be used for this purpose, but starting from Equation 8.7, we can derive the standard error for a comparison. Denoting the difference between the mean scores for two raters, i and i', by $d_{ii'}, = \overline{Y}_{A_i} - \overline{Y}_{A_{j'}}$ we obtain for the variance of the mean difference

$$\sigma^2_{d_{ii'}} = E[\ (\overline{Y}_{A_i} - \overline{Y}_{A_{i'}}) - (A_i - A_{i'})\ ]^2$$

$$= \frac{1}{nt} [n\sigma^2_{A_iB} + n\sigma^2_{A_{i'}B} + 2\sigma^2], \tag{8.11}$$

since the expectation of $d^2_{ii'}$ is

$$E(d^2_{ii'}) = (A_i - A_{i'})^2 + \frac{1}{nt} [n\sigma^2_{A_iB} + n\sigma^2_{A_{i'}B} + 2\sigma^2]. \tag{8.12}$$

Therefore, it is apparent that an estimate of the right side of Equation 8.11 will provide the *MSE* for an *F* and its square root the *SE* for a *t* test of the comparison. Just as for the SE^2 of an individual mean, estimates of the variances on the right sides of Equation 8.11 and 8.12 can be obtained from analyses of the simple effect of *B* at levels i and i' of *A*. In the special case of $s=2$ (two raters in the example), we have:

$$\sigma^2_{A_iB} = \sigma^2_{A_{i'}B} = \sigma^2_{AB}$$

so that the variance and SE^2 of the comparison take the simpler forms

$$\sigma^2_{d_{ii'}} = \frac{1}{nt}(n\sigma^2_{AB} + \sigma^2) \qquad (8.13)$$

and

$$\sigma^2_{d_{ii'}} = SE^2_{d_{ii'}} = \frac{2}{nt}MS_{AB}. \qquad (8.14)$$

It might be mentioned that versions of the random effects model have been proposed in which $\sigma^2_{A_iB}$ is assumed equal to σ^2_{AB} for all i in general so that Equations 8.13 and 8.14 hold regardless of the number of levels of A in the design (e.g., Arnold, 1981, pp. 266–267). This property is convenient, but as is often the case, the price is a strong assumption that is hard to verify empirically and that may rarely be satisfied.

The methods used in the treatment of comparisons between two means can readily be extended to contrasts over sets of means. Thus, if we wished to compare particular subsets of raters, we would define a contrast over levels of A,

$$C = \Sigma_i \lambda_i \overline{Y}_i, \qquad (8.15)$$

where

$$\Sigma_i \lambda_i = 0.$$

Then, employing the usual method, we could derive

$$E(C^2) = (\Sigma_i \lambda_i A_i)^2 + \frac{1}{t}\sigma^2_{AB}\Sigma_i \lambda_i^2 + \frac{1}{nt}\sigma^2 \Sigma_i \lambda_i^2 \qquad (8.16)$$

and

$$SE^2_C = \frac{MS_{AB}}{nt}\Sigma \lambda_i^2. \qquad (8.17)$$

The simplest mixed (RF) design

We will round out our treatment of two-way factorial designs with the case in which one factor has random and one factor fixed effects. By way of introduction, I want to emphasize that mixed designs, including both random and fixed effects, raise difficult problems of interpretation, especially when the number of factors is large. In many cases, there are no ways of forming test statistics that follow the F distribution, and all tests are approximations. In a few instances, sampling studies have shown that the approximations are usually good, but in more cases the goodness of approximation is unknown. In all cases, the assumptions about variances and covariances are important, and deviations from the assumptions can yield seriously invalid tests. Nonetheless, mixed designs, especially designs including subjects as a random factor, are very common in psychological research, and we need to be able to deal with them as intelligently as possible. Continuing our general strategy, we will start with a thorough treatment of the two-way design and develop some methods that will be useful in dealing with larger designs. A general principle is that overall tests are especially vulnerable to deviations from the assumptions, whereas comparisons between means and other one-degree-of-freedom contrasts are more robust, especially if the error estimates are based on the same subsets of data as the comparisons or contrasts.

It does not matter whether the fixed effects of the mixed designs are associated with the rows or the columns of the two-way design, and we will arbitrarily assign the random effects to the rows (factor A) and the fixed effects to the columns (factor B); thus, our model for the analysis is

$$Y_{ijk} = \mu + A_i + \beta_j + A\beta_{ij} + e_{ij}. \tag{8.18}$$

In terms of the Raters and Schools example, we assume that we have drawn a sample of s raters and wish to generalize our conclusions to the whole population but are obtaining ratings only of applications from a particular set of t schools and expect to limit our conclusions to these schools.

The *EMS* table for this design involves no new ideas and takes the following form:

Source	df	MS	EMS
A	$s-1$	MS_A	$nt\sigma_A^2 + \sigma^2$
B	$t-1$	MS_B	$ns\theta_\beta^2 + n\sigma_{A\beta}^2 + \sigma^2$
AB	$(s-1)(t-1)$	MS_{AB}	$n\sigma_{A\beta}^2 + \sigma^2$
Within	$st(n-1)$	MS_W	σ^2

A numerical example may help make it entirely clear why the interaction variance, $\sigma_{A\beta}^2$, appears in the row for the random factor but not in the row for the fixed factor. We will let $s=t=2$, and choose the parameter values

$$\mu = 100 \qquad A_2 = 4$$
$$a_1 = -6 \qquad \beta_2 = -10$$
$$\beta_1 = 10 \qquad A\beta_1 = -3$$
$$A\beta_{11} = 3 \qquad A\beta_{22} = 4 \ .$$
$$A\beta_2 = -4$$

By definition, the values of β_j have to sum to zero, because the population includes only the two effects β_1 and β_2, and similarly the interaction effects have to add to zero when we sum over the subscript j, corresponding to the fixed factor. However, A_1 and A_2 are just two values sampled from the population of A effects, and these values need not sum to zero or any other particular total. With regard to the interaction effects $A\beta_{ij}$, there are only two possible values of j, corresponding to the levels of the fixed factor, but the values of i are sampled from a larger population.

When we compute row and column means for this example, we obtain the following for the rows:

$$
\begin{array}{lllll}
Y_{11} = 100 & -6 & +10 & +3 \\
Y_{12} = 100 & -6 & -10 & -3 \\
\hline
\overline{Y}_{A_1} = 100 & -6 & 0 & 0
\end{array}
$$

and

$$
\begin{array}{lllll}
Y_{21} = 100 & +4 & +10 & -4 \\
Y_{22} = 100 & +4 & -10 & +4 \\
\hline
\overline{Y}_{A_2} = 100 & +4 & 0 & 0
\end{array}
$$

The values representing B effects and interaction effects do not contribute to the values of the means, and consequently they cannot contribute to the EMS for factor A.

Doing the same exercise for the column means yields the following:

$$
\begin{array}{llll}
Y_{11} = 100 & -6 & +10 & +3 \\
Y_{21} = 100 & +4 & +10 & -4 \\
\hline
\overline{Y}_{B_1} = 100 & -1 & +10 & -.5
\end{array}
$$

and

$$
\begin{array}{llll}
Y_{12} = 100 & -6 & -10 & -3 \\
Y_{22} = 100 & +4 & -10 & +4 \\
\hline
\overline{Y}_{B_2} = 100 & -1 & -10 & +.5
\end{array} \; .
$$

All of the effects contribute to the column means. However, the mean square for factor B depends only on differences between the means, and

$$
\overline{Y}_{B_1} - \overline{Y}_{B_2} = 0 + 0 + 20 - 1.
$$

The B effects and the interaction effects contribute to the difference between means, so θ_β^2 and $\sigma_{A\beta}^2$ both appear in the row for factor B in the EMS table.

Following the same reasoning as in our previous treatments of the FF and RR cases, we see by reference to the RF EMS table that we can test the significance of the A main effect against MS_W, but we must test the B effect by means of

$$
F_{(t-1),\ (s-1)(t-1)} = \frac{MS_B}{MS_{AB}},
$$

and the interaction effect by

$$
F_{(s-1)(t-1),\ st(n-1)} = \frac{MS_{AB}}{MS_W} \; .
$$

Standard errors for means in the RF design are obtained in the same way as for corresponding means in the FF and RR designs, so I will simply list some frequently needed formulas.

For a column (fixed-effect) mean:

$$\overline{Y}_j = \mu + \frac{1}{ns} \sum_{i,k} A_i + \beta_j + \frac{1}{ns} \sum_{i,k} A\beta_{ij} + \frac{1}{ns} \sum_{i,k} e_{ijk} \tag{8.19}$$

$$= \mu + \overline{A}_{(j)} + \beta_j + \overline{A\beta}_{-j} + \overline{e}_{-j-} ,$$

where the subscript (j) indicates that the mean is for level j of factor B. The variance of the mean is

$$\sigma_{\overline{Y}_j}^2 = \frac{1}{s} (\sigma_A^2 + \sigma_{A\beta_{-j}}^2 + \frac{\sigma^2}{n}), \tag{8.20}$$

the quantity in parentheses being estimable by $MS_{A(B)}$ in an ANOVA for the simple effect of A at level j of B. For a difference between two column means:

$$d_{jj'} = \overline{Y}_j - \overline{Y}_{j'} ,$$

$$\sigma_{d_{jj'}}^2 = \frac{1}{ns} (n\sigma_{A\beta_{-j}}^2 + n\sigma_{A\beta_{-j'}}^2 + 2\sigma^2) , \tag{8.21}$$

the terms within the parentheses being estimable by the interaction mean squares in ANOVAs for simple effects of A at levels j and j' of B.

If $t=2$, Equation 8.21 reduces to

$$\sigma_{d_{jj'}}^2 = \frac{2}{ns} (\sigma_{A\beta}^2 + \sigma^2) , \tag{8.22}$$

and the quantity in parentheses can be estimated by the MS_{AB} in the overall ANOVA.

For a contrast over column means:

$$C = \sum_j \lambda_j \overline{Y}_j, \tag{8.23}$$

$$\sigma_C^2 = \frac{1}{ns} (n\sigma_{A\beta}^2 + \sigma^2) \sum_j \lambda_j^2 \tag{8.24}$$

$$\hat{\sigma}_C^2 = SE_C^2 = \frac{1}{ns} \, MS_{AB} \sum_j \lambda_j^2 \; . \tag{8.25}$$

For a row (random effect treated as fixed) mean:

$$\overline{Y}_{A_i} = \mu + A_i + \frac{1}{nt} \sum_{j,k} e_{ijk} \; , \tag{8.26}$$

there being no terms in β or $A\beta$, because

$$\sum_j \beta_j = \sum_j A\beta_{ij} = 0.$$

Furthermore,

$$\sigma_{\overline{Y}_{A_i}}^2 = \frac{\sigma^2}{nt} \; , \tag{8.27}$$

with the estimate

$$\hat{\sigma}_{\overline{Y}_{A_i}}^2 = SE_{\overline{Y}_{A_i}}^2 = \frac{MS_W}{nt} \; . \tag{8.28}$$

For a difference between two row (random effects treated as fixed) means: Letting

$$d_{ii'} = \overline{Y}_{A_i} - \overline{Y}_{A_{i'}} \; ,$$

we obtain

$$\sigma_{d_{ii'}}^2 = \frac{2\sigma^2}{ns} \; , \tag{8.29}$$

with the estimate

$$\sigma_{d_{ii'}}^2 = SE_{d_{ii'}}^2 = \frac{2MS_W}{ns} \; , \tag{8.30}$$

For a cell mean (both effects treated as fixed):

$$\bar{Y}_{ij} = \mu + A_i + B_j + AB_{ij} + \frac{1}{n} \sum_k e_{ijk} ; \tag{8.31}$$

the variance of the mean is

$$\sigma^2_{\bar{Y}_{ij}} = \frac{\sigma^2}{n} , \tag{8.32}$$

and its estimator is

$$\hat{\sigma}^2_{\bar{Y}_{ij}} = SE^2_{\bar{Y}_{ij}} = \frac{MS_W}{n} . \tag{8.33}$$

APPENDIX

Derivation of the *EMS* for the simple effect of factor *A* at level 1 of factor *B* in the *FF* design:

The *SS* for this effect is simply the *SS* between levels for a one-way ANOVA over the data in Column 1 of the design table, denoted $SS_A(1)$,

$$SS_{A(1)} = n\sum_i (\bar{Y}_{i1} - \bar{Y}_{-1})^2 . \tag{A1}$$

In terms of the model, the means on the right can be expressed as

$$\bar{Y}_{i1} = \frac{1}{n} \sum_k Y_{i1k} = \frac{1}{n} \sum_k (\mu + \alpha_i + \beta_1 + \alpha\beta_{i1} + e_{i1k})$$

$$= \mu + \alpha_i + \beta_1 + \alpha\beta_{i1} + \bar{e}_{i1-}$$

and

$$\bar{Y}_{-1} = \frac{1}{ns} \sum_{i,k} Y_{i1k} = \frac{1}{ns} \sum_{i,k} (\mu + \alpha_i + \beta_1 + \alpha\beta_{i1} + e_{i1k})$$

$$= \mu + \beta_1 + \bar{e}_{-1-} ,$$

because

$$\sum_i \alpha\beta_{i1} = 0.$$

Substituting these expressions into Equation A1 yields

$$SS_{A(1)} = n\sum_i(\alpha_i + \alpha\beta_{i1} + \bar{e}_{i1-} - \bar{e}_{-1-})^2$$
$$= n\,\Sigma\,(\alpha i + \alpha\beta_{i1})^2 + \sigma^2\,(n-1)\,.$$

Therefore, the EMS for the simple effect is

$$E(MS_{A(1)}) = n\,\theta^2_{\alpha(1)} + \sigma^2\,, \tag{A2}$$

where

$$\theta^2_{\alpha(1)} = \frac{1}{s-1}\,\Sigma(\alpha_i + \alpha\beta_{i1})^2\,. \tag{A3}$$

Equation A3 defines the population measure of effect size for the simple effect analogously to θ^2_α, the population measure of the A main effect in the full ANOVA.

9 Repeated-Measures Designs

Many psychological research designs, most in some domains, employ "repeated measures" on the same subjects. The term repeated measures signifies that each subject is tested under more than one condition. In a two-way design, for example, each subject might be tested at all levels of one of the factors or at all levels of both factors. Designs including repeated measures on any factor require special treatment in order to avoid lumping consistent individual differences between subjects with experimental error. To illustrate, suppose that each member of a group of ten subjects were tested for performance in reading highway signs under each of five lighting conditions. If the data were analyzed with the simple fixed-effects ANOVA discussed in Chapter 6, the summary table would take the following form:

Source	df	Mean Square	EMS
Between conditions	4	MS_B	$10\theta_\alpha^2 + \sigma^2$
Within	45	MS_W	σ^2

and one would test for the effect of conditions by $F = MS_B/MS_W$. The problem with this analysis is that there might well be consistent individual differences in visual acuity that would cause some subjects to score higher than others across all conditions, and the acuity effects would be lumped with effects of experimental error in MS_W, which is being used as the error estimate for the F test. The model equation for the ANOVA,

$$Y_{ij} = \mu + \alpha_i + e_{ij}$$

(Equation 6.1 of Chapter 6), allows only for condition effects and random error. In order to provide for representation of the acuity differences in the model, and, thus, to enable separation of their effects from error effects in the ANOVA, one would turn to a repeated-measures model.

Now the investigator has a new problem — there is no single, standard model for repeated measures. The approach I shall follow is to interpret subjects in a repeated measures design simply as an additional factor, which may be a source of either fixed or random effects (normally the latter). Following this approach, we would augment the model equation for the study of lighting conditions by terms representing the effects of consistent subject differences.

$$Y_{ij} = \mu + \alpha_i + P_j + \alpha P_{ij} + e_{ij} , \qquad (9.1)$$

where P_j denotes the consistent effect associated with subject j, interpreted as a random effect with variance σ_P^2, because the outcome tree for the significance test represents the results of a sequence of replications of the experiment with the same lighting conditions but new random samples of subjects.

An advantage of this way of handling repeated measures is that no new concepts or assumptions are required beyond those applicable to mixed models in general. The principal alternative approach is always to treat subjects as a fixed effect but to modify the standard definition of error variables (e.g., e_{ij} in Equation 9.1) to allow nonzero intercorrelations of errors across conditions within subjects. The only material difference from the mixed-model approach is that negatively correlated errors are allowed for. Derivations of *EMS* tables and *F* tests under this interpretation are given in Arnold (1981). In actual research, investigators may rarely have occasion to consider the possibility of negatively correlated errors, so the mixed model approach is quite generally serviceable.

REPEATED MEASURES IN COMPUTER PACKAGES

Repeated measure designs are customarily treated as a special category in computer statistical packages, but often with inconvenient restrictions on the combinations of repeated and nonrepeated measure factors that can be handled. By comparing alternative analyses of a particular data set and examining the associated *EMS* tables, I will show that the restrictions can be circumvented and all mean squares needed for a repeated-measures analysis can be obtained from the output of a simple, multifactor, fixed-effects ANOVA. The data I will use for illustrative purposes, presented in Table 9.1, come from an experiment conducted as part of a Harvard University dissertation study (Chaiken, 1987). The experimental situation was the short-term memory search paradigm described in Chapter 1. On each trial of the experiment, the subject is first shown a random sequence of digits (the memory set) and then a test digit (the probe), which may be included or not included in the memory set. The subject's task is to respond to the probe as quickly as possible by pressing a "yes" key signifying that the probe was a member of the memory set or a "no" key signifying that it was not. The data we will use are reaction times (in milliseconds) for response to the probe. The experimental variables were number of digits in the memory set (list length) and nature of the previous trial (test on a positive or negative probe). The same three subjects, P_1, P_2, and P_3, were run under all conditions. For brevity, we will henceforth label the experimental factors as A with three levels (list lengths, 3, 4, and 6) and B with two levels (positive or negative previous trial). The data in Table 9.1 are mean reaction times for each subject over a series of trials on each combination of conditions.

Several ANOVAs have been computed for these data by entering the data in a computer program (Human System Dynamics, ANOVA II; others could have been used as well) with different answers to queries about the design. First, although the same three subjects were run under all conditions, a two-way, completely randomized factorial design (Design 1) with sample size 3 (three scores per cell) was specified. The

Table 9.1
Reaction Times for Three Subjects in Memory Search Study

		B_1	B_2
A_1	P_1	416	436
	P_2	442	482
	P_3	436	460
A_2	P_1	460	465
	P_2	489	506
	P_3	457	467
A_2	P_1	507	503
	P_2	537	545
	P_3	472	482

purpose of this analysis is to enable us to determine whether the error estimate is reduced when we go on to designs that eliminate any consistent individual differences between subjects from the error estimate. The output was the uppermost summary in Table 9.2. Next a request was made for a completely randomized three-way factorial design (Design 2) with subjects as the third factor (C with 3 levels), all three factors being treated as sources of fixed effects. The ANOVA output was the middle summary in Table 9.2. Finally a two-way,

Table 9.2
ANOVA Summary Tables for Memory Search Study

Design 1

Source	SS	df	MS	F	p
A	11681.333	2	5840.667	9.605	.003
B	938.890	1	938.890	1.544	.236
AB	440.446	2	220.223	.362	
W	7297.328	12	608.111		
Total	20357.998	17			

Design 2

Source	SS	df	MS	F	p
A	11681.333	2	5840.667	528.376	<.001
B	938.889	1	938.889	84.937	.001
AB	440.446	2	220.223	19.922	.010
C	5416.333	2	2708.167	244.994	<.001
AC	1675.335	4	418.834	37.890	.003
BC	161.445	2	80.723	7.303	.047
Resid.	44.217	4	11.054		
Total	20357.998	17			

Design 3

Source	SS	df	MS	F	p
Blocks/Subjects	5416.330	2			
A	11681.333	2	5840.667	13.945	.017
Error	1675.330	4	418.834		
B	938.890	1	938.890	11.631	.075
Error	161.447	2	80.724		
AB	440.446	2	220.223	19.924	.010
Resid.	44.211	4	11.053		
Total	20357.997	17			
(Pooled error)	1880.997	10			

repeated-measures design (Design 3) was requested, yielding the lower-most summary in Table 9.2.

A glance at the three ANOVA summaries brings out both some correspondences and some notable differences. The *MS* for factor *A* is the same in all three tables, but its significance ranges from p < .001 to p = .017. The *B* main effect again has the same *MS* in all tables, but its significance ranges from p = .001 to p = .236, and much the same pattern holds for the *AB* interaction. In order to interpret these results, we start with the models associated with the three designs.

For Design 1, the model is

$$Y_{ijk} = \mu + \alpha_i + \beta_j + \alpha\beta_{ij} + e_{ijk} , \tag{9.2}$$

where α_i, β_j, and $\alpha\beta_{ij}$ denote the effects of *A, B,* and their interaction respectively, and e_{ijk} is the error variable, subject to the usual assumptions.

For Design 2, the model is

$$Y_{ijk} = \mu + \alpha_i + \beta_j + \pi_k + \alpha\beta_{ij} + \alpha\pi_{ik} + \beta\pi_{jk} + \alpha\beta\pi_{ijk} + e_{ijk} , \tag{9.3}$$

the new terms, involving π_k, representing the (fixed) subject effect and its interaction with the other factors.

For Design 3, we use a special case of the mixed model,

$$Y_{ijk} = \mu + \alpha_i + \beta_j + \alpha\beta_{ij} + P_k + \alpha P_{ik} + \beta P_{jk} + \alpha\beta P_{ijk} + e_{ijk} , \tag{9.4}$$

where P_k represents the random effect of subject differences. In contrast to Design 2, where subjects were viewed as a source of fixed effects, it is assumed in Design 3 that the subject effect is a random variable with variance σ_P^2. The last two terms on the right of Equation 9.4 involve the same subscripts; therefore, they cannot be separated in the analysis. Thus, the error variance σ^2 cannot be separately estimated from the data in this design — only the composite term $\sigma_P^2 + \sigma^2$ can be estimated, as will become apparent in the *EMS* table. If we had more than one score per subject in each cell of the data table (which actually could be supplied in the full data of Chaiken's study), then it would be possible to estimate σ_P^2 and σ^2 individually. With or without such replication, in Design 3 the variance of a score is

$$\sigma_Y^2 = \sigma_P^2 + \sigma_{\alpha P}^2 + \sigma_{\beta P}^2 + \sigma_{\alpha\beta P}^2 + \sigma^2 , \tag{9.5}$$

in contrast to Designs 1 and 2, where the variance is simply

$$\sigma_Y^2 = \sigma^2 .$$

Proceeding in the usual way, we can derive *EMS* tables for each of these designs, as summarized in Table 9.3. A major point to be illustrated by these analyses is that the user of a statistical package need not be unduly constrained by the labels given to various designs. If we understand the models underlying the analyses, we can generally find alternative ways to get a statistical program to compute the quantities and tests of interest. In Design 1, we have ignored the fact that the scores in the six cells do not represent independent samples of subjects; hence all variation between subjects is allowed to influence the error estimate. The B factor has no significant effect according to the ANOVA summary table, but this conclusion does not seem satisfactory, because in 8 of 9 instances, subjects had longer reaction times under B_2 than under B_1.

In Design 2, we take account of the systematic differences that appear to exist between subjects (Subject 2 having the longest reaction times and Subject 1 the shortest on the average) by defining a factor π to represent subject differences. With the subject effects that inflated the residual (W) mean square in Design 1 removed, the residual mean square in Design 2 is greatly reduced. However, we encounter a new problem. Inspection of the *EMS* table for Design 2 reveals that no valid *F*s can be defined, and, therefore, none of the effects can be tested. One way around this impasse is to modify the model by assuming that the three-way interaction is zero. Then the term $\alpha\beta\pi_{ijk}$ disappears from the right side of Equation 9.3 and so also does the term $\sigma^2_{\alpha\beta\pi}$ in the residual row of the Design 2 *EMS* table. Now all effects can be tested against the residual mean square, and we note that the *F*s for the main effects and interaction are much larger than in Design 2. We must recognize, however, that in Design 2, subjects are regarded as a source of fixed effects, meaning that our conclusions refer only to replications of the experiment with the same subjects.

In Design 3, in contrast, conclusions refer to replications of the experiment in which each involves a new random sample of subjects. With subjects interpreted as a random factor P, the *EMS* table shows that each of the effects should be tested against its interaction with subjects as the error term. The resulting *F*s are less significant than the corresponding ones in Design 1, but they justify generalization of the effect of factor A (list length) and its interaction with factor B to the population of subjects sampled. However, comparison of the ANOVA summary tables and the *EMS* tables for Designs 2 and 3 makes it clear that all of the *F* tests called for in Design 3 could have been computed with the output for Design 2. Once we are clear about the models underlying the designs and their associated *EMS* tables, we can construct the appropriate *F*s to test effects of interest from any program output that provides the needed sums of squares.

Table 9.3
EMS Summaries for the Three Designs Applied to the Chaiken Data

Design 1 Independent Groups (FF)			Design 2 Subjects as a Factor (FFF)			Design 3 Repeated Measures (FFR)		
Source	df	EMS	Source	df	EMS	Source	df	EMS
A	2	$6\theta_\alpha^2 + \sigma^2$	A	2	$6\theta_\alpha^2 + \sigma^2$	A	2	$6\theta_\alpha^2 + 2\sigma_{\alpha P}^2 + \sigma^2$
B	1	$9\theta_\beta^2 + \sigma^2$	B	1	$9\theta_\beta^2 + \sigma^2$	B	1	$9\theta_\beta^2 + 3\sigma_{\beta P}^2 + \sigma^2$
AB	2	$3\theta_{\alpha\beta}^2 + \sigma^2$	AB	2	$3\theta_{\alpha\beta}^2 + \sigma^2$	AB	2	$3\theta_{\alpha\beta}^2 + \sigma_{\alpha\beta P}^2 + \sigma^2$
W	12	σ^2	C	2	$6\theta_\pi^2 + \sigma^2$	P	2	$6\sigma_P^2 + \sigma^2$
			AC	4	$2\theta_{\alpha\pi}^2 + \sigma^2$	AP	4	$2\sigma_{\alpha P}^2 + \sigma^2$
			BC	2	$3\theta_{\beta\pi}^2 + \sigma^2$	BP	2	$3\sigma_{\beta P}^2 + \sigma^2$
			Resid.	4	$\theta_{\alpha\beta\pi}^2 + \sigma^2$	ABP	4	$\sigma_{\alpha\beta P}^2 + \sigma^2$

Note. Entries above the dashed line refer to fixed treatment effects in all three designs, those below to error effects, which may be either fixed or random, involving subjects.

Table 9.4
Expected Mean Squares of Table 9.3 in Shorthand Notation

Design 1			Design 2			Design 3		
Source	*df*	*EMS*	*Source*	*df*	*EMS*	*Source*	*df*	*EMS*
A	2	$\underline{A} + E$	A	2	$\underline{A} + E$	A	2	$\underline{A} + AP + E$
B	1	$\underline{B} + E$	B	1	$\underline{B} + E$	B	1	$\underline{B} + BP + E$
AB	2	$\underline{AB} + E$	AB	2	$\underline{AB} + E$	AB	2	$\underline{AB} + ABP + E$
W	12	E	C	2	$\underline{C} + E$	P	2	$P + E$
			AC	4	$\underline{AC} + E$	AP	4	$AP + E$
			BC	2	$\underline{BC} + E$	BP	2	$BP + E$
			Resid.	4	$\underline{ABC} + E$	ABP	4	$ABP + E$

The usefulness of *EMS* tables to guide the construction of valid *F* tests has perhaps become obvious. It is good procedure for an investigator to write out an *EMS* table for each new design considered, preferably before data are collected, so that it can be determined whether all desired tests can actually be accomplished. For complex designs, however, constructing *EMS* tables can become tedious, and it is often convenient to use a "shorthand" notation like that shown in Table 9.4. The correspondence between terms in Tables 9.3 and 9.4 should be fairly obvious. The notation will be seen to be similar to that used in model specifications in SYSTAT, except for the convention that letters or letter combinations denoting fixed effects are underlined to distinguish them from those denoting random effects. Tables written in this shorthand notation do not suffice for all purposes, but they can serve in place of full tables for the purpose of guiding the construction of *F* tests in balanced designs.

TWO-WAY FACTORIAL DESIGNS

Multifactor designs including repeated measures raise difficult problems of interpretation. Even when some of the factors would ideally be regarded as sources of random effects, the hazards of interpreting overall tests in higher-order mixed designs are so great that it is often advantageous to start an analysis by treating all of the factors as sources of fixed effects and determining whether effects of interest are significant for the specific conditions studied. If the results of this step are negative, one need go no further. If they are positive, one can go on and seek evidence as to whether the findings for the particular levels of random factors studied are generalizable to the populations sampled.

To obtain a pattern that can be extended directly to more complex cases, we will work through the following design fully, making clear the bases for estimates of standard errors and tests of hypotheses. We consider a two-way factorial design with repeated measures on one factor, both factors being treated as sources of fixed effects.

$$B$$

A	Subjects	1	2	.	.	.	.	.	t
1	G_1								
2	G_2								
.									
.									
.									
s	G_S								

The G_k denote groups of n subjects with each subject tested under all levels of factor B. Our model for the design takes the form

$$Y_{ijk} = \mu + \alpha_i + \beta_j + \alpha\beta_{ij} + P_{k:i} + \beta P_{jk:i} + e_{ijk},$$

where $P_{k:i}$ denotes the effect associated with subject k within level i of factor A, having variance σ_P^2, and $BP_{jk:i}$ the interaction of subjects with factor B (within levels of A) whose variance is denoted σ_I^2. The EMS table is as follows:

Source	df	MS	EMS full notation	EMS Shorthand
A	$s-1$	MS_A	$nt\theta_\alpha^2 + t\sigma_P^2 + \sigma^2$	$\underline{A} + P + E$
B	$t-1$	MS_B	$ns\theta_\beta^2 + \sigma_I^2 + \sigma^2$	$\underline{B} + BP{:}A + E$
AB	$(s-1)(t-1)$	MS_{AB}	$n\theta_{\alpha\beta}^2 + \sigma_I^2 + \sigma^2$	$\underline{AB} + BP{:}A + E$
$P{:}A$	$s(n-1)$	$MS_{P:A}$	$t\sigma_P^2 + \sigma^2$	$P + E$
$BP{:}A$	$s(t-1)(n-1)$	$MS_{BP:A}$	$\sigma_I^2 + \sigma^2$	$BP{:}A + E$

Reference to the shorthand EMS entries shows us immediately that $MS_{BP:A}$ is the appropriate error term for testing the B main effect and the AB interaction, and $MS_{P:A}$ is the appropriate error term for the A main effect. If our analysis is done by one of the standard statistical packages, these will be the error terms indicated in the printout. Furthermore, some programs, including BMDP, will report a statistic labeled "Greenhouse-Geisser ϵ," which estimates the degree to which the data deviate from the assumptions of the model concerning homogeneity of variances and covariances (technically the deviation from "compound symmetry" of the covariance matrix). A value near 1.0 indicates that the assumptions are well satisfied; smaller values signify deviations. One can correct for deviations to some extent by multiplying the df for the numerator and denominator mean squares of an F by ϵ and using the corrected df (interpolating in the F table if necessary) when looking up the significance of the F. This correction is needed, only if the numerator of the F has more than one df, one reason why contrasts can often be more safely interpreted than overall Fs in repeated-measure designs.

Unfortunately the standard errors that are needed as soon as we wish to go beyond overall effects and deal with specific questions or hypotheses about various aspects of the data are not generally provided by the computer printouts. However, by making good use of the model for the design, we can usually figure out how to calculate standard errors that use the mean squares or sums of squares that are presented in the printout.

Comparisons between treatment means are usually the easiest cases to handle. It will be recalled from Chapter 3 that the SE^2 of any contrast among means is given by

$$SE_C^2 = MS_{\text{error}} \frac{\Sigma\lambda^2}{N},\tag{9.6}$$

where MS_{error} is the appropriate error mean square, and N is the number of scores entering into each mean. For a comparison between any two means for levels of factor A in this design, shorthand expressions for the two means, in terms of the model, are

$$\overline{Y}_{A_i} = A_i + \overline{P}_i + \overline{e}_i$$

and

$$\overline{Y}_{A_{i'}} = A_{i'} + \overline{P}_{i'} + \overline{e}_{i'},$$

the notation $\overline{P}_i$ signifying the sample mean of the subject effect at level i, and so on. If there is no A effect ($A_i = A_{i'} = 0$), then the expected value of the squared difference between means will include only subject and error effects, so we expect the $MS_{P:A}$ to be the appropriate choice for MS_{error}. In this case, $\Sigma\lambda^2$ is equal to 2, and the number of scores entering into each mean (N in Equation 9.6) is equal to nt, where n is the number of subjects, and t is the number of levels of B, thus, the desired SE^2 would be

$$SE^2_{d_{ii'}} = \frac{2}{nt} MS_{P:A} .$$

If we carry out the complete derivation, we find

$$\sigma^2_{d_{ii'}} = \frac{2}{nt} (t\sigma^2_P + \sigma^2) ,$$

where

$$d_{ii'} = \overline{Y}_{A_i} - \overline{Y}_{A_{i'}} .$$

Reference to the summary table shows that $MS_{P:A}$ is the appropriate estimator for $t\sigma^2_P + \sigma^2$, confirming the correctness of the informal result. In exactly the same way, we can show that for a comparison between two means for levels of factor B, the SE^2 is equal to $MS_{BP:A}\frac{2}{ns}$. For contrasts involving more than two levels of either factor A or factor B, these results are easily adapted simply by replacing the 2 in the numerator with the appropriate value of $\Sigma\lambda^2$.

It should be noted that in many texts, including Winer (1971), the SE^2 for a comparison of two means is given a rather misleading label, such as $SE^2_{\overline{A}}$ or $\hat{\sigma}^2_{\overline{A}}$. The correct interpretation is that the quantity so labeled is to be substituted for MS_{error}/N in the formula for SE^2_C of a contrast.

Standard errors of individual treatment means can be a little trickier. In this design, means for levels of factor A present no special problem. The variability of the mean for a particular level of A, say $\overline{Y}_{A_i}$, over replications of the experiment is due entirely to variation in $\overline{P}_i$ and $\overline{e}_i$, so we expect our estimate of SE^2 to come from the row of the summary table for $P:A$, that is,

$$SE^2_{\overline{Y}_{A_i}} = \frac{MS_{P:A}}{nt} ,$$

which is correct, because

$$\sigma^2_{\overline{Y}_{A_i}} = \frac{1}{nt} (t\sigma^2_P + \sigma^2) .$$

For a factor B mean, the shorthand expression is

$$\overline{Y}_{B_j} = B_j + \overline{P} + \overline{I}_j + \overline{E}_j , \qquad (9.7)$$

so we expect $\sigma^2_{\overline{Y}_{B_j}}$ to depend on P, I, and E. That conclusion is correct, but we cannot get an expression for SE^2 by this informal route, for a derivation of $\sigma^2_{\overline{Y}_{B_j}}$ yields

$$\sigma^2_{\overline{Y}_{B_j}} = \frac{1}{ns} \left(\sigma^2_P + \frac{t-1}{t} \sigma^2_I + \sigma^2 \right) . \tag{9.8}$$

If we look to the summary table for estimators of the various terms (σ^2_P, σ^2_I, σ^2), we see that none are available. We can circumnavigate the problem, however, if (referring to the design table) we notice that the variability of $\overline{Y}_{B_j}$ over replications of the experiment is due entirely to variation in the samples of scores in the cells $A_1B_j, A_2B_j, \ldots A_sB_j$, which we might describe as "mean square within cells," or MS_W. The expected value of this MS is

$$E(MS_W) = \sigma^2_P + \frac{t-1}{t} \sigma^2_I + \sigma^2 , \tag{9.9}$$

so MS_W/ns is exactly what we need as an estimator for $\sigma^2_{\overline{Y}_{B_j}}$. Incidentally MS_W is also the appropriate error mean square for a test of the simple effect of factor A at any level j of factor B. Further, reference to the summary table plus a little algebra shows that in terms of sums of squares,

$$E(SS_W) = E(SS_{P:A} + SS_{BP:A}) , \tag{9.10}$$

so the sums of squares on the right added together and divided by the combined df ($st \, (n-1)$) gives us MS_W without any additional computation.

If each subject is run under all conditions in a fixed-effects factorial design, the pattern of expected mean squares is especially simple. Consider a two-way design with each of n subjects run under each combination of factors A and B. In shorthand notation, the summary table is as follows:

Source	df	MS	EMS
A	$s-1$	MS_A	$\overline{A} + AP + E$
B	$t-1$	MS_B	$\overline{B} + BP + E$
AB	$(s-1)(t-1)$	MS_{AB}	$\overline{AB} + ABP + E$
P	$n-1$	MS_P	$P + E$
AP	$(s-1)(n-1)$	MS_{AP}	$AP + E$
BP	$(t-1)(n-1)$	MS_{BP}	$BP + E$
ABP	$(s-1)(t-1)(n-1)$	MS_{ABP}	$ABP + E$

The proper Fs for main effects and interactions are obvious. In a computer printout from a statistical package, AP would be listed as "error"   below the A main effect, BP below B, and ABP below AB.

The pattern of expected mean squares extends directly to larger numbers of factors. For a three-way design, for example, we would have

Source	df	MS	EMS
A	$r-1$	MS_A	$\underline{A} + AP + E$
B	$s-1$	MS_B	$\underline{B} + BP + E$
C	$t-1$	MS_C	$\underline{C} + CP + E$
P	$n-1$	MS_P	$P + E$
AB	$(r-1)(s-1)$	MS_{AB}	$\underline{AB} + ABP + E$
.			
.			
.			
ABC	$(r-1)(s-1)(t-1)$	MS_{ABC}	$\underline{ABC} + ABCP + E$
AP	$(r-1)(n-1)$	MS_{AP}	$AP + E$
.			
.			
.			
ABP	$(r-1)(s-1)(n-1)$	MS_{ABP}	$ABP + E$

and so on.

The SE^2 for a comparison of means for two levels of factor A is $2/nt \; MS_{AP}$ for the two-way design and $2/nst \; MS_{AP}$ for the three-way design, and the expressions for comparisons on the other factors are similar.

PROBLEMS WITH MORE COMPLEX MIXED DESIGNS

Even minor complication of mixed designs can give rise to situations in which the design that seems most plausible for a research problem proves on analysis to provide no valid tests for effects of primary interest. To illustrate, consider a type of design that arises in psycholinguistic research:

	Treatments (Word Categories)		
	Noun	*Verb*	*Adjective*
Subjects	$n_1 \; n_2 \ldots n_w$	$v_1 \; v_2 \ldots v_w$	$a_1 \; a_2 \ldots a_w$
1			
2			
.			
.			
.			
s			

This design (adapted from one used in simulation studies by Wickens and Keppel, 1983) represents a hypothetical experiment in which an investigator wishes to compare three types of words with respect to some performance variable, for example, the speed with which they can be categorized when presented one at a time to subjects on a display screen. There are three experimental effects to be dealt with in an analysis of the data — the effect of treatments (differences among word categories), the effect of differences among words within categories, and the effect of individual differences among subjects. Treatments would surely be viewed as a source of fixed effects and subjects of random effects, but the effects of different words within categories might be viewed as either fixed or random. Presumably the investigator would want to generalize any conclusions about word or category effects to the populations of words sampled, so we will start by defining a model for the experiment on the assumption that word effects are random. The model equation is

$$Y_{ijk} = \mu + \alpha_i + W_{j:i} + P_k + \alpha P_{ik} + WP_{jk:i} + e_{ijk} , \qquad (9.11)$$

where α_i denotes the treatment (category) effect, $W_{j:i}$ the effect of words within categories, and P_k the effect associated with subject k. The notation $W_{j:i}$ and $WP_{jk:i}$ reflects the fact that different words were used in the different categories (for which reason there is no interaction of words with treatments). With shorthand notation for the *EMS* entries, the ANOVA summary table takes the following form:

Source		df	MS	EMS
Treatments	A	$t-1$	MS_A	$\underline{A}$ + $W{:}A$ + AP + $(W{:}A)P$ + E
Words	$W{:}A$	$t(w-1)$	$MS_{W{:}A}$	$W{:}A$ + P + $(W{:}A)P$ + E
Subjects	P	$s-1$	MS_P	P + $(W{:}A)P$ + E
Interaction	AP	$(t-1)(s-1)$	MS_{AP}	AP + $(W{:}A)P$ + E
Residual	$(W{:}A)P$	$t(s-1)(s-1)$	$MS_{(W{:}A)P}$	$(W{:}A)P$ + E

Here the example has been generalized slightly to allow any numbers of treatments, $t > 2$. The terms that go into the *EMS* entries are abbreviations for the terms that would appear in a full table. Each row includes a term for the corresponding effect, terms for its interactions with random factors, and the usual error term (E being our abbreviation for σ^2). The first row, written out in full in standard notation, would be

$$sw\theta_\alpha^2 + so_{W:A}^2 + wo_{AP}^2 + \sigma_{(W:A)P}^2 + \sigma^2 \, .$$

Presumably the main purpose of the analysis is to test for treatment effects, but a glance at the *EMS* entries shows that no *F* is available, because there is no other row in the table that includes all of the random effects in the Treatments row. We can test the *AP* interaction, using $MS_{(W:A)P}$ as the error term, but the interaction is not likely to be of major interest. One way to cope with this problem, introduced to psychologists by Clark (1973), is to compute a "Quasi *F*," for the treatment effect. Examining the *EMS* column of the table, we note that, if we add together the entries for MS_{AP} and $MS_{W:A}$ and subtract those for $MS_{(W:A)P}$, the combination of terms we come out with, $W:A + AP + (W:A)P + E$, is exactly what we need. The ratio

$$F_Q = \frac{MS_A}{MS_{AP} + MS_{W:A} - MS_{(W:A)P}}$$

has the necessary property of an *F* that, if there were no treatment effect (that is, if all of the α_i were equal to zero), the expected values of the numerator and denominator would be equal. This Quasi *F* is said to be distributed approximately as a true *F* having *df* that are estimated by some rather complex formulas (given in the Appendix). Unfortunately however, we generally cannot know how good the approximation is. A sampling study reported by Wickens and Keppel (1983) suggests that for this design, the Quasi *F* test is generally conservative to the point of being woefully lacking in power. This shortcoming is serious, because there is not much point in doing research if we cannot expect to detect treatment effects. Another approach suggested by Clark, the computation of what he calls a "minimum *F*," has the same shortcomings. For this design, the minimum *F* for treatments would be

$$F_{\min} = \frac{MS_A}{Ms_{AP} + MS_{W:A}} \, .$$

Adding together the entries in the *EMS* table for the mean squares in the denominator, we see that the combination of terms is larger in value than the combination that should appear in the denominator of an *F*, so the value of $F_{\min}$ will be too small (in the sense that using it with estimated *df* will result in accepting the null hypothesis too often). Therefore, like the Quasi *F*, $F_{\min}$ is conservative but lacking in power.

Given the shortcomings of the suggested remedies for the lack of an appropriate test of the treatment effect in this design, where shall we turn for a practical solution? Perhaps the simplest way out is to give up on the assumption that words exert random effects and plan to limit our conclusions from the study to the particular words used. With this modification, our shorthand *EMS* table takes the form

Source	EMS
A	$A + AP + E$
$W{:}A$	$W{:}A + (W{:}A)P + E$
P	$P + E$
AP	$AP + E$
$(W{:}A)P$	$(W{:}A)P + E$

Now we can test the treatment effect, with MS_{AP} as the error term. If this effect proves significant but the word ($W{:}A$) effect nonsignificant, we might feel little concern about the generality of our result. If the word effect proves significant, we will need to limit our conclusion to the specific materials tested until the experiment is replicated with new samples of words.

An alternative plan is to divide the sample of words in each category into two or more subsets, thus, in effect, producing replications, and plan to conclude that the treatment effect is generalizable to the population of words sampled only if the interaction of A with "replications" is not significant, or alternatively, if the simple effect of treatments (corrected for experiment-wide error rate) proves significant within each subset. If, for example, we choose two subsets, the portion of the design table for any treatment, say the noun category in the example, would be as follows:

Subjects	Nouns	
	Set 1	Set 2
1	$n_{11} \ldots n_{1w}$	$n_{21} \ldots n_{2w}$
2		
.		
.		
.		
s		

and the modified summary table, assuming random effects only for subjects, would be the following:

Source	df	MS	EMS
A	$t-1$	MS_A	$A + AP + E$
S	1	MS_S	$S + SP + E$
AS	$t-1$	MS_{AS}	$AS + ASP + E$
W:AS	$2t(w-1)$	$MS_{W:AS}$	$W{:}AS + (W{:}AS)P + E$
P	$s-1$	MS_P	$P + E$
SP	$s-1$	MS_{SP}	$SP + E$
AP	$(t-1)(s-1)$	MS_{AP}	$AP + E$
ASP	$(t-1)(s-1)$	MS_{ASP}	$ASP + E$
WP:AS	$2t(w-1)(s-1)$	$MS_{(W:AS)P}$	$(W{:}AS)P + E$

In effect, the experiment has been replicated with the same treatments and subjects but new selections of words within categories, so S can be viewed as denoting replications. For this tactic to be promising, we might need some pilot work to estimate the word subset sizes that would be needed to provide satisfactory power. Our decision strategy is to test the A main effect against MS_{AP}, but to conclude that significant effect is generalizable beyond the particular samples of words used only if a test of MS_{AS} against MS_{ASP} indicates no significant AS interaction.

This analysis should alert us to the fact that, in general, there are no pat solutions to the problems that arise with mixed designs. What can always be done, however, is to limit the conclusions we draw from a study to those that can be justified by the design.

APPENDIX

Quasi Fs for Subjects $\times$ Treatments $\times$ Words Design

1. $F' = \dfrac{MS_A}{MS_{AP} + MS_W + MS_{WP}} = \dfrac{u}{w + x - v}$,

with df denom. $= \dfrac{(w + x - v)^2}{\dfrac{w^2}{n_w} + \dfrac{x^2}{n_x} + \dfrac{v^2}{n_v}}$,

where $n_i = df$ for term i.

2. $F' = \dfrac{MS_A + MS_{WP}}{MS_{AP} + MS_W} = \dfrac{u + v}{w + x}$,

with df num. $= \dfrac{(u + v)^2}{\dfrac{u^2}{n_u} + \dfrac{v^2}{n_v}}$

and df denom. $= \dfrac{(w + x)^2}{\dfrac{w^2}{n_w} + \dfrac{x^2}{n_x}}$.

10 Unbalanced Designs and Nonorthogonality

CELL MEANS AND EFFECT MODELS

As a preliminary to the treatment of unbalanced designs, we need to discuss some aspects of the general linear model that have been bypassed for convenience in the preceding chapters. The treatments of ANOVA for balanced designs in Chapters 8 and 9 have been based on what is termed the Effects form of the linear model. The reason for the label *Effects* is apparent in Equation 6.1, the model equation for a one-way, fixed-effects design, repeated here,

$$Y_{ij} = \mu + \alpha_j + e_{ij}, \tag{10.1}$$

where the term α_j represents a quantity that would have to be added to or subtracted from the population mean μ, to obtain the population mean for condition j, which may be termed μ_j. The difference between μ_j and μ is then a measure of the effect of the experimental treatment associated with condition j. In the *Cell Means* form of the linear model, the model equation for the one-way design is simply

$$Y_{ij} = \mu_j + e_{ij}. \tag{10.2}$$

It might seem that, because $\mu_j = \mu + \alpha_j$, the two versions of the model are exactly equivalent except for the choice of notation. However, it can be easily seen that equivalence does not hold in general. To make this point, let us consider the simple case of $j = 2$. Then in the Cell Means model, the expected values of scores in conditions 1 and 2 are

$$E(\overline{Y}_1) = \mu_1$$

and

$$E(\overline{Y}_2) = \mu_2 ,$$

so the sample means for conditions 1 and 2 provide unbiased estimators of the parameters μ_1 and μ_2. In the Effects model, however, the expected values are

$$E(\overline{Y}_1) = \mu + \alpha_1$$

and

$$E(\overline{Y}_2) = \mu + \alpha_2$$

Now we have a problem in that there are three population parameters in the Effects model, but the data of an experiment yield only the two independent sample means $\overline{Y}_1$ and $\overline{Y}_2$. Thus, we can estimate the quantities $\mu + \alpha_1$ and $\mu + \alpha_2$, or by subtracting one quantity from the other, the difference $\alpha_1 - \alpha_2$, but we cannot estimate μ, α_1, or α_2 separately. The import of this conclusion is that, if we cannot obtain a suitable estimate of a parameter from the data of an experiment, then we cannot define an F test for a hypothesis about the value of that parameter.

The standard solution to this problem is to augment the Effects model with assumptions that restrict the possible values of the parameters. For the case of Equation 10.1, the added assumption usually employed is

$$\Sigma_j \alpha_j = 0. \tag{10.3}$$

With this restriction, $\alpha_1 = -\alpha_2$ when $j = 2$, and we have for the expectations of sample means

$$E(\overline{Y}_1) = \mu + \alpha_1$$

and

$$E(\overline{Y}_2) = \mu + \alpha_2 = \mu - \alpha_1 ,$$

Therefore, having estimated $\mu + \alpha_1$ by $\overline{Y}_1$ and $\mu - \alpha_1$ by $\overline{Y}_2$, we obtain

$$\hat{\mu} = \frac{\overline{Y}_1 + \overline{Y}_2}{2}$$

as an estimate of μ and

$$\hat{\alpha}_1 = \frac{\overline{Y}_1 - \overline{Y}_2}{2}$$

as an estimate of α_1. For the restricted version of the Effects model then, we may be able to define tests of hypotheses about the values of the parameters μ and α_j. Because of the estimation problem, the restricted form of the Effects model was assumed throughout Chapters 6 through 9 (and is assumed in most textbook presentations of ANOVA).

Analogous considerations obtain for two-way and higher-order designs. For the case of two factors, A and B, the cell means model for a crossed (factorial) design is

$$Y_{ijk} = \mu_{ij} + e_{ijk}, \tag{10.4}$$

where i and j index levels of A and B respectively, and obviously each of the parameters μ_{ij} can be estimated by the corresponding sample mean $\overline{Y}_{ij}$. Ordinarily one is interested in hypotheses concerning the population row means μ_{i-}, *and column means,* μ_{-j}, and these can be estimated by the corresponding row and column sample means $\overline{Y}_{i-}$ and $\overline{Y}_{-j}$.

The Effects model corresponding to Equation 10.4 has the model equation

$$Y_{ijk} = \mu + \alpha_i + \beta_j + \alpha\beta_{ij} + e_{ijk}, \tag{10.5}$$

previously introduced as Equation 8.1 of Chapter 8. In the general case of this Effects model (i.e., no restrictions on the parameter values), we again run into the problem that there are more parameters than observation equations, so the parameters μ, α_i, β_j, and $\alpha\beta_{ij}$, cannot be estimated separately, only combinations like $\mu + \beta_1$ or $\mu + \alpha_1 + \alpha\beta_{11}$, and, therefore, there is no possibility of testing hypotheses about the individual parameters. This constraint is very strong, implying, for example, that although our prime concern in a study were with the significance of the effect of factor A, we could not hope to test the hypothesis that the α_i are equal to zero.

As in the one-way design, the Effects model becomes useful only when augmented by assumptions that reduce the number of independent parameters to equality with the number of independent observation equations. The assumptions usually added (as in Chapter 8) are

$$\Sigma_i \alpha_i = 0$$

$$\Sigma_j \beta_j = 0$$

and

$$\Sigma_i \alpha \beta_{ij} = \Sigma_j \alpha \beta_{ij} = 0 \ ,$$

termed for brevity the Σ restrictions. In a two-way design with two levels of each factor, for example, there are four independent cell means available to enter into equations for parameter estimation, and the restrictions reduce the nine independent parameters of the model (μ, α_1, α_2, β_1, β_2, $\alpha\beta_{11}$, $\alpha\beta_{12}$, $\alpha\beta_{21}$, and $\alpha\beta_{22}$) to four. The choice of four independent parameters is to a degree arbitrary but might reasonably be μ, α_1, β_1, and $\alpha\beta_{11}$.

It should be noted that in a (very typical) research situation in which the investigator has the option of choosing the number of levels of each factor, even the restricted Effects model does not allow estimation of the population mean, μ, in any general sense, for the estimable parameter, μ, of the model is simply the mean of the population cell means. Thus, if in otherwise comparable studies of teaching methods, one investigator chose to compare methods M_1, M_2 and M_3 in schools S_1 and S_2, whereas another investigator chose to investigate methods M_1 and M_2 in schools S_1, S_2, and S_3, estimates of the parameter μ of the restricted Effects model could not be expected to be the same (even on the average) in the two studies.

In applications of the restricted Effects model, it is not possible to define an empirically meaningful concept of a population mean distinct from the parameter μ, defined as the mean of the population cell means for the treatment combinations actually studied in a given situation.

The Effects model is useless for most purposes of hypothesis testing unless augmented by the Σ restrictions, and even then enables tests of hypotheses about effects of separate experimental factors only under a limited set of conditions; therefore, one might wonder why it is the model of choice in most textbooks and, so far as I know, all manuals for statistical computer packages. The answers are evidently that historically the Effects model became familiar earlier than the Cell Means model and that it is more convenient for expressing assumptions and hypotheses about effects of experimental variables. The limitations of the Effects model have not become as familiar as its convenient features, but they deserve at least as close attention.

ANALYSES OF UNBALANCED DESIGNS

In all of the treatments of ANOVA and regression in Chapters 7 through 9, orthogonality has been assumed. *Orthogonality* means essentially that independent variables are uncorrelated. Nonorthogonality arises in two principal ways. In a regression analysis with two or more independent variables, the values of the independent variables may have nonzero correlations, even if the design is balanced (an especially common problem in ANCOVA). In a multiclassification ANOVA design, nonorthogonality is usually the result of imbalance. The focus of this chapter is the handling of unbalanced ANOVA designs.

We speak of an unbalanced design if the cell frequencies for the various conditions are not equal and do not form a simple pattern in which the entries in rows and columns are in the same proportions. An easy way to check on whether an apparently orthogonal design (e.g., a standard factorial design) is unbalanced is to code the data for input to a program like SYSTAT and then run correlations on the columns for the independent variables. If the design is balanced, the correlations will be zero; if the design is unbalanced, the correlations will be nonzero, indicating that the factors entering into the design are not orthogonal.

The importance of balance versus unbalance in designs is that all of the simple properties of ANOVA/regression hold only for balanced designs. That is, in balanced designs, the various component sums of squares in the standard ANOVA output add up to the total sum of squares; the various tests of effects and interactions refer directly to hypotheses about parameters of the population (for example, the test for row effects is a test of the hypothesis that the parameters representing effects of the row factor in the population are all equal to zero). In unbalanced designs, the sums of squares in the standard output are not additive (thus, for example, one cannot obtain a sum of squares for interaction by subtracting the other sums of squares from the total), and the tests of various effects may not be related in any simple way to population parameters. In fact, it is often very difficult to determine what meaningful hypothesis is being tested by an F for a main effect.

Fortunately the effects of nonorthogonality of factors are quantitatively graded and become serious for practical purposes only if unbalance is fairly extreme. If, for example, one loses only a case here and there from a fair sized data set, it is sensible to ignore the imbalance[1] and simply run the desired ANOVA or regression analysis on a program like SYSTAT or BMDP and interpret the output in the usual way. Some statisticians say that ANOVA should be used only with balanced designs. However, that admonition is unnecessarily purist, and the practical researcher can often get at least some useful information from unbalanced data sets. The following sections will outline a strategy that can be used with unbalanced data sets and indicate both what can be accomplished by way of meaningful interpretations and what limitations cannot be overcome.

There is a large literature on unbalanced designs, notable for the many controversies about recommended procedures and interpretations. Many of the disagreements arise from failures to specify precisely the hypotheses being tested and the models assumed to underlie analyses in particular cases. Most of the problems of interpretation arise only if there are at least two factors in a design, and essentially no new issues arise when the number of factors is larger, so the following examination of the available methods for testing various hypotheses will focus on a two-way classification with unequal frequencies. I will limit consideration to fixed effects and independent samples of subjects in the treatment combinations. The family of models that will provide our theoretical framework can be summarized in short-hand notation as follows

$$Y = M + A + B + A^*B + E \tag{10.6}$$

$$Y = M + A + B + E \tag{10.7}$$

$$Y = M + A + E \tag{10.8}$$

$$Y = M + B + E \tag{10.9}$$

$$Y = M + E . \tag{10.10}$$

In each case, Y is the dependent variable, M the mean, E the error term, and the remaining terms the row, column, and interaction effects. These equations can be interpreted analogously to the model specifications in SYSTAT. (SYSTAT differs only in using CONSTANT in place

---

[1]Or to estimate the missing value by one of the standard methods (see, e.g., Snedecor & Cochran, 1980, pp. 274–276).

of M and dropping the error term.)[2] When we are analyzing a balanced design, we need only run the analysis corresponding to Equation 10.6; all of the effects are orthogonal, and the sums of squares (SS) for the components add up to SS_{tot}. However, for an unbalanced design, the analysis has to be carried out by means of comparisons between models, more precisely, comparisons between the SS for effects and error resulting from fitting different models to the given data set.

Random and nonrandom attrition

To deal with unbalanced data sets, we need to consider carefully how the subjects were sampled and the reasons for losses of subjects from the different cells of the design. In the balanced case, we customarily assume that some prescribed number n of subjects is sampled from the reference population for each cell of the design. In unbalanced cases, it sometimes is reasonable to assume that the sampling plan is the same but that there was some probability p that the score for each subject would be lost from the analysis. (The subject failed to appear on schedule; the subject failed to meet some performance criterion; the score was lost because of an equipment error.) Thus, over a series of replications of the experiment, the distribution of numbers of cases per cell would vary entirely randomly from replication to replication. Conclusions from the experiment refer to replicability of the results over such a series of replications, and hypotheses tested refer to population parameters such as μ_{ij} or α_i. When these assumptions are satisfied, we speak of random attrition.

Under some circumstances, random attrition is not plausible, and it makes better sense to turn to an alternative that I will designate nonrandom attrition. In this version, the sampling plan is the same, but the loss probabilities for individual scores are not independent of the cells. For example, in the hypothetical study involving Raters and Schools that was analyzed in Chapter 8, applications from different schools might have different probabilities of getting GREs completed in time to make the applications eligible for rating, or some raters might be more interested in some schools than others and, thus, be more likely to get the ratings done for the preferred schools. Both of these factors would lead to the loss of scores from some cells of the design, but the probability of loss would not be independent of the particular row-

---

[2]Equation 10.6 corresponds to the general linear model equation for this design,

$$y_{ijk} = \mu + \alpha_i + \beta_j + \alpha\beta_{ij} + e_{ijk},$$

and Equations 10.7 through 10.10 to the submodels obtained by omitting various terms.

column combination. Similarly in a memory experiment involving, for example, level of incentives and retention interval, losses of scores might be more likely at the longer retention intervals and at the lower incentives, again leading to cell frequencies that would not vary independently of the combinations of conditions. Under these circumstances, replication of an experiment will tend to yield cell frequencies n_{ij} similar to those of the original experiment. In the simplest (and the only practical) sampling model for this type of situation, it is assumed that the n_{ij}s are fixed in value over replications, either in absolute terms or as proportions of the total N. In the analysis, one is interested in testing hypotheses about population means weighted by the n_{ij}.

A strategy for analyses

Regardless of the sampling assumptions, it is a good practice to start with a one-way ANOVA over all of the cells of the design. In a two-way classification with a rows and b columns, we simply define a dummy factor C with levels $C_1, C_2, \ldots C_{ab}$. Using SYSTAT, we would then run the ANOVA with the model command $Y = \text{constant} + C$. The unequal cell frequencies raise no complications for the one-way ANOVA, and an F for the C effect tests the hypothesis that all of the cell means (μ_{ij}) are equal in the population sampled. If this F is not significant, the analysis ordinarily terminates (unless the decision strategy includes planned contrasts). If the F is significant, and the investigator wishes to evaluate main effects of the A and B factors, the next step is to test for interaction, because the presence or absence of interaction in the population is a critical determiner of the hypotheses that can be tested in further analyses.

The test for interaction is obtained by estimating the full model for the design in a standard ANOVA with any least-squares based program — for the details of computation, see Searle (1987) or Winer (1971). In SYSTAT, the model command would correspond to Equation 10.6, and an F for MS_{AB} against MS_{Error} would test the hypothesis that all of the population interaction parameters are equal to zero. Beyond any interest in the interaction per se, we wish to use this test as a basis for deciding whether we are justified in testing for main effects with a model that does not include an interaction term. We wish to take this step only if we are quite confident that there is no interaction, so we set a lax criterion, typically a .25 significance level.

Analysis of factorial main effects
under random attrition

If the test for interaction is significant, then no tests are possible for hypotheses referring to population main effects (e.g., hypotheses such as all $\alpha_i = 0$ or all $\beta_j = 0$ in the general model). However, we can test the hypothesis that all of the row means are equal in the population, for example, that the quantities

$$\mu_{i-} = \frac{1}{b} \Sigma_j \, \mu_{ij}$$

are equal for all i, or the analogous hypothesis for column means. The simplest way to carry out these tests is to run an ANOVA program for the model of Equation 10.6 with one of the main effect terms omitted. In SYSTAT, the model command needed in evaluating the A main effect would be $Y = \text{constant} + B + A*B$, and the difference between the SS_E in the output for this submodel and the SS_E for the full model (in SYSTAT, $Y = \text{constant} + A + B + A*B$) provides an estimate of SS_A. Alternatively the same estimate could be obtained by multiplying the SS_{Tot} obtained in the one-way ANOVA[3] by the difference between the R^2 in the output for the full model and the R^2 for the submodel. An F for the MS_A obtained from the estimate against the MS_E from the full model (or the one-way) output provides a test of the hypothesis that all of the row means are equal in the population (that is, $\mu_{1-} = \mu_{2-} = \dots = \mu_{a-}$). A test for the analogous hypothesis about column means would be obtained by using the submodel $Y = \text{constant} + A + A*B$.

Note again, however, that a test of a main effect, say A, obtained in this manner does not justify any conclusion regarding the existence of a main effect of the experimental factor corresponding to A in the design independently of the other factor, for the factors are not orthogonal in this case, and the observed A effect may be due in part to the influence of the B factor. All we conclude, for example, if the F test for A is significant, is that a replication of the experiment under similar conditions could be expected to yield a similar observed effect on the row means. We do not in particular have any basis for rejecting the hypothesis that all $\alpha_i = 0$.

The results of this analysis would be approximated by the "unweighted means" analysis described by Howell (1987, ch. 13) and Rosenthal and Rosnow (1985, pp. 268–272). However, it has become so easy to carry out an exact analysis by means of a computer program like SYSTAT or BMDP that there is not much point in using approximations.

If the test for interaction (together with any other relevant information that is available) proves to justify the assumption of no interaction in the

---

[3]We could not use for this purpose the SS_{Tot} obtained from the two-way ANOVA, because it will generally be smaller than the correct SS_{Tot} in the case of an unbalanced design.

population, then it is possible to test for main effects. The procedure is to start with the no-interaction model corresponding to Equation 10.7 and compare the output with those for the submodels corresponding to Equations 10.8 and 10.9. The difference between the R^2 for Equations 10.7 and 10.9 multiplied by SS_{Tot} (or simply the difference between the SS_E for the two outputs) yields an estimate of SS_A, and an F for the MS_A against the MS_E tests the hypothesis of no main effect for A (i.e., all α_i are equal). A similar computation of course yields an analogous test for the B main effect.

Analysis of factorial main effects under nonrandom attrition

Finally, if we are assuming nonrandom attrition, then regardless of the outcome of the test for interaction, we can test hypotheses that all weighted row means or all weighted column means are equal by comparing the R^2 values (or SS_E) obtained from estimation of the model corresponding to Equation 10.8 or Equation 10.9 respectively with the value obtained for Equation 10.10. The F for the MS_A or MS_B so computed tests the appropriate hypothesis about weighted population means.

Examples of unbalanced factorial designs

This outline of the available models and procedures for dealing with unbalanced data sets is rather abstract, therefore, we turn now to some illustrations of procedures and problems of interpretation in terms of numerical examples. For a start, we will use the data set for which the number of scores (n_{ij}) and the cell mean for each combination of factors A and B are shown in matrix I of Table 10.1. The n_{ij} were chosen to produce a moderately unbalanced data set, and the scores were computed from Equation 10.6 with the population mean equal to 10: the row effects equal to 1, 0, and -1; the column effects all equal to 0; the interaction effects equal to

$$
\begin{array}{ccc}
1 & -.5 & -.5 \\
-.5 & 1 & -.5 \\
-.5 & -.5 & 1 \\
\end{array}
$$
,

in the format of the data matrix in Table 10.1, and σ^2_{error} equal to 1.0.

The SYSTAT output for a one-way ANOVA over all cells of the design is as follows:

Source	df	SS	F	p
Between cells	8	50.72	19.4	$< .001$
Within	27	8.84		
Total	35	59.56		

Table 10.1
Unbalanced Data Sets Generated by Models With Known
Population Parameters

I.

	B_1	B_2	B_3	*Weighted*	*Unweighted*
A_1	6	6	3		.
	12.18	10.55	10.47	11.19	11.07
A_2	4	4	3		
	9.32	11.02	9.93	10.10	10.09
A_3	2	6	2		
	8.70	8.58	10.35	8.96	9.21
Weighted	10.65	9.93	10.24		
Unweighted	10.07	10.05	10.25		

II.

	B_1	B_2	B_3	*Weighted*	*Unweighted*
A_1	8	2	2		
	11.85	11.20	10.45	11.51	11.17
A_2	2	2	2		
	10.05	11.20	8.75	10.00	10.00
A_3	2	6	10		
	9.50	8.88	9.94	9.54	9.44
Weighted	11.16	9.81	9.84		
Unweighted	10.47	10.43	9.71		

III.

	B_1	B_2	B_3	*Weighted*	*Unweighted*
A_1	8	3	2		
	10.85	11.57	11.20	11.07	11.21
A_2	2	8	2		
	10.30	10.29	10.65	10.35	10.41
A_3	2	3	6		
	9.00	8.90	9.02	8.98	8.97
Weighted	10.45	10.27	9.78		
Unweighted	10.05	10.25	10.29		

The Between-cells effect being highly significant, we reject the hypothesis that all of the μ_{ij} are equal and proceed to an analysis of row and column effects.

First, assuming random attrition, we compute a full two-way ANOVA for the model of Equation 10.6 and obtain the following output:

Source	df	SS	F	p
A	2	17.58	26.80	<.001
B	2	.22	.33	ns
A*B	4	19.85	15.15	.001
Error	27	8.84		
		46.49		

The computation was done with SYSTAT, but BMDP and many other programs would yield the same output. As expected in view of the nonorthogonality produced by the unequal cell sizes, the SS for main effects, interaction, and error do not add up to SS_{Tot} obtained from the one-way ANOVA. The entry for Error is the correct SS_{within}, and it can be shown that the entry for $A*B$ is the correct, least squares estimate of the interaction SS; however, the SS for main effects have shrunk as a consequence of the correlation of A and B with each other and with $A*B$ in the unbalanced data set. The Fs for A and B effects lead to the correct conclusions about the population means — we reject all μ_{i-} equal but accept all μ_{-j} equal; no conclusions about the parameters of α_i or β_j are justified (although in this case it happens that we would correctly reject $\alpha_1 = \alpha_2 = \alpha_3 = 0$ and accept $\beta_1 = \beta_2 = \beta_3 = 0$).

If we instead assume nonrandom attrition, we start out the same way but would use only the $A*B$ row in the full two-way ANOVA. We compare the fits of Equations 10.8 and 10.9 with Equation 10.10 (done expeditiously by means of the SYSTAT model commands $Y = $ Constant $+ A$; $Y = $ Constant $+ B$; and $Y = $ Constant) to estimate the effects of each factor ignoring the other. The outputs are as follows:

Source	df	SS	F	p
A	2	30.01	16.76	.001
Error	33	29.55		
and				
B	2	3.54	1.04	ns
Error	33	56.02		

These are equivalent to one-way ANOVAs on the rows and columns of the design and indicate that we can reject the hypothesis of equal weighted row means but accept the hypothesis of equal weighted column means.

To see what can happen with a still more unbalanced data set, consider Data Set II in Table 10.1. The population parameters are the same as those of Data Set I, but the n_{ij} vary more extremely. Estimation of Equation 10.6 yields the following SYSTAT output:

Source	df	SS	F	p
A	2	14.26	31.2	< .001
B	2	2.91	6.4	.005
A*B	4	12.12	13.3	< .001
Error	27	6.17		
Total		35.46		

The SS_{Tot} has shrunk even more dramatically in this case, the correct value for a one-way ANOVA being 48.19. If, in spite of the highly significant interaction, we look at the test of main effects, we find that we can reject the hypotheses of equal row means and equal column means. Again however, we are not justified in making any inference about the parameters α_i and β_j in the design. If we were to proceed blindly to draw conclusions about these parameters, we would incorrectly reject the null hypothesis for both.

The gist of these results is to point out the conclusion that when evidence of interaction is present in an unbalanced data set, no inferences can safely be drawn about population main effects. Tests of specific contrasts between cells that are prescribed by a priori hypotheses are still appropriate, assuming appropriate Bonferroni adjustments for multiple tests on the same data set.

For contrast, we will now look at an unbalanced data set with no interaction in the population. Set III of Table 10.1 was generated by the same model as Sets I and II, except that all of the interaction effects were set equal to 0. A one-way ANOVA over the 9 cells of the design yields the following:

Source	df	SS	F	p
Cells	8	27.82	12.18	< .001
Error	27	7.71		
Total		35.53		

and because the F is highly significant, we proceed to examine more specific effects. Starting with the assumption of random attrition, we estimate the full model of Equation 10.6, obtaining the following:

Source	df	SS	F	p
A	2	23.42	41.00	< .001
B	2	.27	.47	ns
A*B	4	.87	.76	ns
Error	27	7.71		
Total		32.27		

which leads to correct conclusions about interaction and about row and column means in the population. Interaction can confidently be ruled out, thus, we can proceed to estimate the reduced model of Equation 10.7. The model command $Y = \text{Constant} + A + B$ to SYSTAT produces the following output:

Source	df	SS	F	p
A	2	24.38	44.10	< .001
B	2	.54	.97	ns
Error	31	8.58		

We find that we can accept the hypothesis of a main effect of factor A in the population (i.e., reject all α_i equal).

If we should be interested in nonrandom attrition, estimation of the models corresponding to Equations 10.8, 10.9, and 10.10 yields appropriate estimates of SS_A and SS_B for tests of hypotheses about weighted row means and weighted column means respectively—

Source	df	SS	F	p
A	2	23.41	35.1	< .001
Error	33	11.07		
and				
B	2	12.21	9.1	.001
Error	33	22.21		

The output lends some confidence to the expectation that the observed row and column effects would hold up over replications of the experiment with the same cell frequencies.

Contrasts on means are computed for unbalanced data exactly as for balanced data. If, for example, we wished to compare the mean of column 1 with the average of the other two column means in Data Set I, the contrast would be

$$C = 2(10.65) - 9.93 - 10.24 = 1.13 .$$

The standard error of the contrast would, however, have to take account of the unequal ns. The formula for SE_C^2 given in Equation 4.9 of Chapter 4 becomes

$$SE_C^2 = MSE \sum_j \frac{\lambda_j^2}{n_j} , \text{ which in this example would be}$$

$$SE_C^2 = .327 \left(\frac{2^2}{12} + \frac{1^2}{16} + \frac{1^2}{8} \right) = .327 \, (.5208) = .170,$$

the value of MSE being taken from the ANOVA output. It will be noted that the generalized formula for SE_C^2 reduces to the one in Chapter 4 in the special case when all of the n_j are equal.

Similarly the contribution of a contrast to the treatment sum of squares has to take account of unequal ns. The formula given in Equation 4.12 of Chapter 4 becomes

$$SS_C = C^2 / \sum_j \frac{\lambda_j^2}{n_j} , \text{ which in this example would be}$$

$$SS_C = \frac{1.13^2}{.5208} = 2.452 .$$

Again the general formula reduces to the one given earlier in the special case of equal ns.

ANALYSIS OF A NESTED DESIGN

I will illustrate a simple case of nested classification with the data shown in Table 10.2. The data represent a hypothetical study intended to compare achievement scores (Y) in two courses, each of which has multiple sections handled by different assistants. We are interested in any

Table 10.2
Data for a Nested Design

Course	Section	Score (Y)
C_1	S_1	5
		9
	S_2	10
		8
	S_3	10
		8
C_2		2
	S_4	1
		6
		3
	S_5	3
		7

differences in mean achievement between courses and any differences among sections within courses. If the design were balanced (that is if all cells had equal numbers of cases), our model equation would be

$$Y_{ijk} = \mu + \alpha_i + \beta_{j:i} + e_{k:i,j}, \tag{10.11}$$

where α_i denotes the effect associated with course C_i and $\beta_{j:i}$ the effect associated with section j within course C_i. Owing to the imbalance, all of the parameters in Equation 10.11 cannot be estimated from the data, and the model equation should be rewritten in terms of the Cell Means model—

$$Y_{ijk} = \mu_{ij} + e_{k:i,j}, \tag{10.12}$$

where μ_{ij} denotes the population mean for section j of course i.

Now we need to deal with a rather confusing technicality. Although the different effects represented in Equation 10.11 cannot be estimated separately, the instruction to a program like SYSTAT or BMPD nonetheless has to be given in the same format as for a balanced design. Thus, the model equation submitted to SYSTAT takes the form

$$Y = M + C + S(1) + S(2), \tag{10.13}$$

where M is a constant, C the course effect, $S(1)$ the effect of sections within Course 1, and $S(2)$ the effect of sections within Course 2.

The ANOVA output for the data of Table 10.2 is as follows:

Source	df	SS	F	p
C	1	3.8	1.01	ns
S:C	3	60.0	5.38	.03
Error	7	26.0		

We note that because of the unbalance in the design, the sums of squares in this output do not add up to SS_T. The SS for error is the same as SS_W from the one-way ANOVA, and the SS for the first and second rows of the table are the values obtained by the methods just described. The total sum of squares and the R^2 for the full model are obtained, just as for a crossed design, by running a one-way ANOVA over all five cells. This analysis yields for the data of Table 10.2 a sum of squares between cells of $SS_B = 84$ and a sum of squares within of $SS_W = 26$, a total of $SS_T = 110$. To test the hypothesis that the population means for sections ($\mu_{j:i}$) are equal within courses, we compare the full model of Equation 10.12 with the reduced model

$$Y_{ik} = \mu_i + e_{k:i}, \tag{10.14}$$

obtained by setting $\mu_{ij} = \mu_i$ for all j. The sum of squares needed for the numerator of the F test is obtained by subtracting the SS_W for the full model from the SS_W for the reduced model; the sum of squares for the denominator is the SS_W for the full model.

The sum of squares for differences between course means can be obtained by computing the sum of squared deviations of the course means from the grand mean as in a balanced design but with the individual terms weighted by harmonic means of the n_{ij}, that is,

$$SS_C = \Sigma_i \, b_i n_i^{(h)} \, (\overline{Y}_i - \overline{Y})^2, \tag{10.15}$$

where b_i is the number of levels within C_i, and $n_i^{(h)}$ is the harmonic mean over j of the n_{ij}. The term $\overline{Y}_i$ in Equation 10.15 is the arithmetic mean over j of $\overline{Y}_{ij}$ and $\overline{Y}$ is the mean of the $\overline{Y}_i$ weighted by $n_i^{(h)}$. The ratio of MS_C to MS_W provides an F test of the hypothesis that the population means for the courses are equal.

In case there is interest in the assumption of nonrandom attrition, an ANOVA corresponding to the equation

$$Y = M + C \tag{10.16}$$

with the following output

Source	df	SS	F	p
C	1	24	2.79	.13
Error	10	86		

can be used to test the hypothesis that the weighted means for levels of C are equal. It might be noted in this connection that, if the test of $MS_{S:C}$ in the full ANOVA leads to acceptance of the null hypothesis, then the F for MS_C in this ANOVA can be interpreted as testing the hypothesis that all of the population means for levels of C (i.e., μ_i) are equal.

AN UNBALANCED ANALYSIS OF COVARIANCE

An unbalanced design including an ANOVA over a categorical variable together with a regression effect on a quantitative variable will be illustrated in terms of the data in Table 10.3. The treatments are three instructional conditions; the Y scores are performance measures at the end of a period of instruction, and the X values are scores on a pretest. The analysis is easily done, and problems arise only in the interpretation. Our purpose is to evaluate the treatment effects adjusted for any effect of the covariate (X). The desired adjustment is readily obtained with any program that handles a combined ANOVA and regression. With SYSTAT, the model equation is

$$Y = \text{Constant} + T + X \tag{10.17}$$

corresponding to the statistical model

$$Y_{ij} = \mu_i + \beta X_{ij} + e_{ij} , \tag{10.18}$$

Table 10.3
Data for an Analysis of Covariance

			Treatment (T)			
	1		2		3	
Y	X	Y	X	Y	X
74	3	76	2	87	3
68	4	80	4	91	7
77	5				

where $\mu\alpha_i$ is the population mean for treatment i, and β is the slope constant for the regression of Y on X. The SYSTAT output is as follows:

Source	df	SS
T	2	243.19
X	1	18.75
Error	3	39.25

which yields an F for treatments significant at the .05 level. The sum of squares for T can be calculated by multiplying the total sum of squares (368.0, obtainable from a one-way ANOVA over levels of T) by the difference between the R^2 for the full model and the R^2 for the model including only the constant and the covariate. The F computed from this sum of squares tests the hypothesis that all of the treatment means are equal (that is, i.e., $\mu_1 = \mu_2 = \mu_3$). The sum of squares for X is obtainable by multiplying the total sum of squares by the difference between the R^2 for the full model and the R^2 for the model including only the constant and T, and the resulting F tests the hypothesis that β is equal to 0. This analysis will serve to reemphasize the point made earlier that analyses of covariance do not require special programs but rather can be accomplished by the same methods used for ANOVA and regression in general.

References

Arnold, S. F. (1981). *The theory of linear models and multivariate Analysis*. New York: Wiley.

Chaiken, S. R. (1987). Scanning and retrieval residues in short-term and long-term recognition tasks. Doctoral dissertation, Harvard University.

Clark, H. H. (1973). The language-as-fixed-effect fallacy: A critique of language statistics in psychological research. *Journal of Verbal Learning and Verbal Behavior, 12*, 335–359.

Dunteman, G. H. (1984). *Introduction to multivariate analysis*. Beverly Hills, CA: Sage.

Estes, W. K., Campbell, J. A., Hatsopoulos, N., & Hurwitz, J. B. (1989). Base-rate effects in Category learning: A comparison of parallel network and memory storage-retrieval models. *Journal of Experimental Psychology*: *Learning, Memory, and Cognition, 15*, 556–571.

Finn, J. D. (1974). *A general model for multivariate analysis*. New York: Holt, Rinehart, and Winston.

Graybill, F. A. (1961). *An introduction to linear statistical models*. New York: McGraw-Hill.

Harris, R. J. (1985). *A primer of multivariate statistics* (2nd. ed). New York: Academic Press.

Hays, W. L. (1988). *Statistics* (4th ed). New York: Holt, Rinehart, and Winston.

Hildebrand, D. K. (1986). *Statistical thinking for behavioral scientists*. Boston: Duxbury.

Howell, D. C. (1987). *Statistical methods for psychology* (2nd ed). Boston: Duxbury.

Hurlburt, R. T., & Spiegel, D. K. (1976). Dependence of F ratios sharing a common denominator mean square. *The American Statistician, 30*, 74–76.

Kirk, R. E. (1982). *Experimental design: Procedures for the behavioral sciences* (2nd ed). Monterey, CA: Brooks/Cole.

Loftus, G. R., & Loftus, E. F. (1988). *Essence of statistics* (2nd ed). New York: Knopf.

Rosenthal, R. & Rosnow, R. L. (1985). *Contrast analysis: Focused comparisons in the analysis of variance*. Cambridge: Cambridge University Press.

Searle, S. R. (1987). *Linear models for unbalanced data.* New York: Wiley.

Snedecor, G. W., & Cochran, W. G. (1980). *Statistical methods* (7th ed). Ames, IA: Iowa State University Press.

Sternberg, S. (1966). High-speed scanning in human memory. *Science, 153,* 652–654.

Wickens, T. D., & Keppel, G. (1983). On the choice of design and of test statistic in the analysis of experiments with sampled materials. *Journal of Verbal Learning and Verbal Behavior, 22,* 296–309.

Wilkinson, L. (1986). *SYSTAT: The system for statistics.* Evanston, IL: SYSTAT, Inc.

Winer, B. J. (1971). *Statistical principles in experimental design* (2nd ed). New York: McGraw-Hill.

Author Index

Subject Index